THE HAMMURABI CODE

AND THE SINAITIC LEGISLATION

WITH

A COMPLETE TRANSLATION OF THE GREAT
BABYLONIAN INSCRIPTION DISCOVERED AT SUSA

BY

CHILPERIC EDWARDS

AUTHOR OF "THE WITNESS OF ASSYRIA," ETC.

[Issued for the Rationalist Press Association, Limited]

WATTS & CO.,
17, JOHNSON'S COURT, FLEET STREET, LONDON, E.C.
1904

THE HAMMURABI CODE

WATTS AND CO., PRINTERS,
17, JOHNSON'S COURT, FLEET STREET, LONDON, E.C.

HAMMURABI ADORING THE SUN-GOD

PREFACE

———

THE object of the present work is to provide a complete and careful translation of the whole of the great Babylonian inscription containing the Laws of Hammurabi, and to bring together in a brief form all the known facts connected with the period of Babylonian history to which it belongs. As, moreover, many persons will be interested in tracing out the dependence of the Mosaic Laws upon the Babylonian legislation, a chapter has been devoted to that subject. Quite independently, however, of its service in discounting arrogant claims in regard to the originality or excellence of the Jewish Pentateuch, the Code of Hammurabi is destined to be of the utmost value to the student of the history of civilisation, and the evolution of Semitic Law. It may even be found eventually that the influence of the Babylonian Code extended beyond the Semitic boundary, and that it has modified the legal ideas of distant peoples; but as yet it is too early to verify any such suggestion. In any case, however, the age, the extent, and the remarkable state of preservation of this venerable monument of antiquity combine to entitle it to the respect and consideration of every thinking being.

The following pages do not coruscate with ingenious speculations upon the origin of the Hammurabi dynasty, as the writer totally fails to see that that has anything to do with the legal enactments. It may, however, be mentioned that some scholars have claimed that certain of the *successors* of Hammurabi bore names which exhibited grammatical forms foreign to the Semitic-Babylonian tongue; and they have argued that his dynasty must therefore be of foreign

origin. One school is anxious to connect
the line with Northern Arabia, the other
with Canaan, and both adduce linguistic
reasons for their choice. Without entering
into these precarious hypotheses, it may
be sufficient to remark that we have no
evidence whatever as to the *grammatical*
peculiarities of the languages spoken in
Arabia or Canaan during the era of Hammurabi—that is to say, before 2000 B.C. The
idioms of Arabic and Hebrew may have been
very different at that early date to what they
became in their classical periods. Furthermore, in most countries proper names exhibit
uncommon or obsolete grammatical forms,
for the simple reason that the names are
handed down through several generations,
and thus are really relics of earlier modes of
speech ; so that the unusual form of some
of the names of Hammurabi's family may
eventually prove to be of this character, and
there will be no excuse for doubting the
Babylonian origin of his race. Leaving

such conjectures on one side, however, it can hardly be disputed that the Laws themselves manifest their specifically Babylonian origin. They contemplate a country with a numerous settled population, where the art of writing is in common use, where agriculture is associated with irrigation upon a large scale, and where ships and navigation play an important part. These points are combined in no other ancient Semitic land; they can only be referred to Babylonia. Mere questions of dynasty are consequently irrelevant. The legislation is only intelligible as a product of Babylonian soil; and as Babylonian culture was of ancient date, and was entirely derived from the still earlier civilisation of the Akkadians, who themselves appear to have had codes of law (see Appendix C), it seems quite unnecessary to insist upon the obvious fact that Babylonian jurisprudence is prior to all other Semitic law or custom of which we have any certain knowledge.

It will, further, be observed that the ensuing

chapters are not besprinkled with the name of "Abraham." The reasons for ignoring this worthy are stated in Appendix B.

In regard to the question of chronology, the author has, in Appendix A, quoted all the evidence that exists for determining the date of Hammurabi. It will be seen that this evidence does not enable us to fix the exact year of that monarch; but it is sufficient to indicate the general period at which he flourished.

C. E.

CONTENTS

CHAPTER I.

THE DISCOVERY OF THE CODE

OUR first introduction to the legal practice of the ancient Babylonians was in 1854, when Mr. W. K. Loftus disinterred a number of clay tablets from the mound of Tell Sifr, which covers the remains of some old city whose name is still unknown. These tablets were found to be "contracts"—that is to say, records of business transactions, effected during the reigns of three monarchs, Rim-Sin, Hammurabi, and Samsu-iluna; but it was many years before the scholars of Europe could thoroughly explain these records, for the cuneiform writing was of a peculiar type, and the language was full of unknown technical expressions. It was not until the Berlin Congress of Orientalists, in 1882, that Dr. P. Strassmaier gave a really satisfactory rendering of them. Meanwhile, material has accumulated. The British Museum in London, the Louvre at Paris, and the Museums of Berlin, Constantinople, and Philadelphia, all contain large collections of "contract tablets," besides a great many scattered in private hands. The efforts of scholars have been chiefly directed to the elucidation of the historical texts, which are not only easier, but also of more immediate interest ; and the polite literature of the Babylonians has also been largely studied. Of late years, however, Babylonian jurisprudence has been receiving the attention of a small but enthusiastic band of workers, among the best known of whom are Dr. Oppert, Dr. F. E. Peiser, and Dr. Bruno Meissner, the results of whose labours have been summarised in an able (though somewhat highly coloured) fashion by Professor G. Maspero in the ninth chapter of his *Dawn of Civilisation* (London, 1894).

In the British Museum there are three or four fragments of tablets from the library of Assurbanipal, king of Assyria (668 to 626 B.C.), which appeared to contain portions of a code of laws. These fragments had long been remarked, and had even been spoken of as the Code of Assurbanipal. Dr. Meissner, however, who had subjected the fragments to considerable study, was struck by their agreement in style and language with the remains of the early Babylonian period ; and in 1898 he suggested that the "Code" to which these tablets belonged would probably be found to go back to the time of the first Babylonian Dynasty. In February, 1899, the celebrated Dr. Delitzsch, in discussing Meissner's remarks,[1] wrote as follows :—

"That the collection of laws in question originated in the period of the first Babylonian Dynasty is certainly a legitimate assumption of Meissner's. It may further be conjectured that no other than Hammurabi himself, the founder of the Babylonian Empire, gave the command to unify the laws and ordinances then current into one Code of Law. Were the tablets from the library of Assurbanipal complete, they would undoubtedly be of extreme value for the history of comparative law."

This was written in the early part of 1899; and in the course of the article he called the presumed collection of Babylonian laws the *Code Hammourabi*, in allusion to the famous *Code Napoleon*, which has had such an enormous influence upon modern European Law. Within three years the conjecture of Dr.

---

[1] "Zur juristischen Litteratur Babyloniens," von Friedrich Delitzsch—*Beiträge zur Assyriologie*, band iv. (February, 1899), p. 80.

Delitzsch was converted into a certainty by the discovery of the complete Code of Laws, with the original proclamation of King Hammurabi.

The laurels of this discovery fall to the French. In 1897 the French Government deputed M. J. de Morgan to open excavations upon the site of Susa, the ancient city of the Persian kings, for purposes of historical investigation. A day or two before the end of December, 1901, the workmen came upon a large fragment of black diorite. A few days later two other fragments were unearthed, and the three pieces, when joined together, were found to form a round pillar in the shape of an elongated sugar-loaf, 7ft. 4in. high, 5ft. 4in. in circumference at the top, and 6ft. 2in. at the bottom. Our frontispiece shows the upper part of this pillar, which, it will be seen, bears a bas-relief 26in. high and 24in. broad, representing Hammurabi standing in the presence of Shamash, the Babylonian God of the Sun. The back and front of the pillar are covered with columns of writing in what is called the Archaic Cuneiform character—that is to say, the ancient Babylonian hieroglyphics executed in wedge-shaped lines. In the time of Hammurabi this style of writing was only employed for sculptures and formal inscriptions. The contract tablets and the correspondence of the period were written in a simplified style called the Old Babylonian Cursive, very similar to the Assyrian Cuneiform usually met with in printed books. The clay tablets appear to have been written and read in horizontal lines, running from left to right. But the inscription of Hammurabi is in rows of short columns, the characters in the columns being read from top to bottom, and the columns themselves running from right to left. In fact, the direction of the writing is exactly the same as in Chinese, to which the Archaic Cuneiform bears a remarkable resemblance. The hard stone of which the monument is composed has preserved the original writing with extreme sharpness, and the three fragments fit together so closely that very little is lost by the fractures. The greatest damage has been done to the inscription, not by accident, but by design, for the last five rows of columns upon the front have been purposely scraped out. This erasure was not made because any of the laws were objected to, but because the monarch who removed the pillar from Babylonia to Susa wished to engrave his own name upon it as a trophy of victory. As that portion of the inscription is now irretrievably lost, it is a pity that he did not carry out his design, and thus leave us a record of the vicissitudes and wanderings of the monument. We can, however, form a pretty close guess at the culprit, for M. de Morgan also found on the acropolis of Susa no less than five monuments of Babylonian kings which had been defaced, and the name of Shutruk-Nakhunte added upon them. This individual was king of Elam about 1100 B.C.; and he appears to have overrun Babylonia and sacked several important cities. Thus M. de Morgan had evidently come upon the museum of Shutruk-Nakhunte, where that monarch exhibited the trophies he had brought back from Babylonia in the shape of the most revered memorials of the Babylonian sovereigns. A fragment of another pillar bearing a few lines of the Code was unearthed at the same place.

If the Elamite had completed his design of placing his own name upon Hammurabi's pillar, he might have settled the important question of its original location. The inscription is not quite clear upon this point; for although in the early part of the prologue Hammurabi says, "In Babylon......in E

Saggil......I have written my precious words, upon my pillar; and before my image as King of Justice I have placed it" (xxiv. 63–78), yet at the end we read of "the circuit of this temple of E Babbara" (xxviii. 76). Both Sippara and Larsam possessed temples to the Sun-God, and both temples bore the name of *E Babbara*, "the House of Light" (in Semitic, *Bit Uri*). The explanation seems to be that the original Code of Hammurabi was erected at Babylon, in the great temple of Merodach called E Saggil; but copies were placed in other temples; and this particular pillar, discovered at Susa, was set up either at Larsam or at Sippara.

At any rate, after journeying from Babylonia to Susa, the pillar has made a still longer voyage; and it now stands in Paris, as one of the greatest treasures of the Louvre. The French Government, recognising the importance of the find, has had the whole of the text published in heliogravure, in a magnificent volume entitled *Textes Élamitiques-Sémitiques*, par V. Scheil, O.P. (Paris, 1902), being *tome iv.* of the *Memoires de la Délégation en Perse*. The eight plates in this volume are so exquisitely executed as to place scholars in the same position as if they had the actual inscription before them. Father Scheil transcribed the text, and rendered it into French in the remarkably short space of ten months from its discovery.

As already remarked, five rows of columns are now missing from the base of the monument; and Father Scheil estimates that these contained some thirty-five ordinances. From the remains of the Assyrian copies of the Code in the British Museum, however, he has been able to restore three of these. And it may be of statistical interest to remark here that the fragmentary tablets from the Library of Assurbanipal contain portions of Sections 57, 58, 59, 103, 104, 107, 111, 112, 113, 114, 115, 119, 120, 277–280, according to Father Scheil's enumeration; and about eighty lines of Hammurabi's prologue.[1] The Berlin Museum has two small fragments of the Later Babylonian period (about 550 B.C.), containing portions of Sections 147, 148, 152, 153, 154, 159, 171. So far as these fragments are legible, they agree almost exactly with the text of the Susian pillar.

[1] The latter was only published by the British Museum authorities at the end of 1901. *Proc. Socy. Bib. Arch.*, vol. xxiv., p. 304.

CHAPTER II.

THE LEGAL SYSTEM OF THE BABYLONIANS

IN ancient Babylonia the business of the law was almost exclusively in the hands of the priesthood, for they included in their ranks the scribes, without whom there could be no books and no records. The halls of justice were usually at the gates of the temples, and there the judges, the scribes, and the "elders" assembled. The "elders" appear to have been a permanent body of officials, for the same names appear again and again upon tablets of about the same date; and we may even recognise a gradual rise, or promotion, of individuals to higher ranks.[1] They played much the same part as the "elders" of the Old Testament (as, for instance, Ruth iv. 2, 9), and acted chiefly as official witnesses to the transactions which took place before them. The judges were appointed by the sovereign,

[1] *Assyrian Deeds and Documents,* by the Rev. C. H. W. Johns, M.A. (Cambridge, 1901), vol. ii., p. 47, § 76.

who exercised a rigid supervision over them. Their duties were extremely varied, ranging from the highest criminal trials to the registration of business documents. As we may see by the Code, only written contracts were recognised, and the activity of the courts of registration is evidenced by the enormous numbers of contract tablets which are being continually brought to light. These tablets show the official hand of the scribe, and are usually couched in set technical terms. The nature of the transaction is briefly and clearly recited; it is stated that the parties understand the conditions of the deed, and have taken oath by certain gods; the deities usually being the tutelary gods of the land and the city, accompanied by the name of the reigning sovereign as their earthly representative and the supervisor of the law—in some cases the monarch has even the determinative for deity prefixed to his name. Then follow the names of the elders; or, as they are usually styled by Assyriologists, the "witnesses"; and the document is completed by the addition of the date. In later times the year of the reigning monarch gave the date; but in the early period, to which Hammurabi belongs, they dated the contracts by the most noteworthy incident of the year, as the building of a temple, an inundation, or a battle. Such a tablet, executed in clay by one of the attendant scribes, sometimes further authenticated by seals, or the thumb-nails of the contracting parties, and baked in a small oven for better preservation, thus became a legal record, producible in any court as evidence of the transaction.

In actions at law the contending parties presented themselves at the gate of the temple. We do not know whether there was any power of arrest. The Roman Law of the Twelve Tables directed the plaintiff to summon the defendant in the open street, and, if he did not answer the summons, to convey him before the judge by force ; but whether a private Babylonian could do the same is not clear. In the royal correspondence the king often directs the apprehension of certain persons and their conveyance under custody ; but apparently there was no organised police to undertake such a duty, though there must have been officials to carry out the sentences of the courts. When the parties to the action appeared before the judges, it was usual for them to bring with them the object in dispute and lay it before the god, as in the old Roman

legis actio sacramento.[1] If the object were not
portable, then it was represented by a part of
it—*e.g.,* a clod of earth would represent an
estate, or a brick a house. Oaths were taken
and witnesses examined, and the judge gave
his decision, which was usually recorded upon
a tablet, and copies delivered to the disputants.
A few such legal decisions have been discovered, but hardly sufficient to give us more
precise details of the practice of the Babylonian courts. Difficult cases were referred
to special functionaries, or presidents, and the
sovereign was always the ultimate court of
appeal. In fact, any citizen had the privilege
of appealing direct to the king for justice if he
considered himself to have any legitimate
grievance ; and from the correspondence of
Hammurabi it would appear that such appeals
were always treated with consideration. The
letters prove Hammurabi to have been an
impartial judge, who tolerated no corruption
in his officials. Ever vigilant for the efficient
administration of justice in his realm, he
immediately remitted particulars of any com-
plaint to the viceroy of the district, with
directions to investigate the matter on the

[1] *Beiträge zum altbab. Privatrecht*, von Bruno Meissner
(Leipsic, 1893).

spot, and to send the guilty party to Babylon for chastisement. In one case we see him supporting the claim of a merchant against a *shakkanakku*, or governor, for the repayment of a loan, so that the king was no respecter of persons where justice was concerned. It must not be supposed, however, that Hammurabi was any exception in this respect. We have evidence that his example was followed by his successors, for there is in the British Museum a letter in which two men have appealed to his grandson Abi-eshu', to the effect that they cannot obtain justice in Sippara; and therefore the king has immediately ordered the trial of their case at Babylon.[1] It may be assumed that the monarch himself tried the majority of cases brought before him, and that he took steps to have his judgments carried out. In the cases of parties living at a distance from the capital, the king's decisions were communicated to the governor of the district in which the disputants dwelt.

There was thus every provision for the administration of justice in Babylonia, and adequate and efficient machinery was provided for this purpose throughout the Babylonian

[1] *The Letters and Inscriptions of Hammurabi*, by L. W. King (London, 1900), vol. iii., p. xxxix., ff.

dominions. The legal system was of great antiquity, for we have contracts, etc., dated in the reigns of the kings of Ur, who preceded Hammurabi's dynasty by many centuries; and a few laws have been preserved which, as they are written in the Akkadian language, must be relics of a very ancient body of legislation (see Appendix C). Consequently, although the Code of Hammurabi was probably a great advance in Babylonian jurisprudence, yet the laws themselves were not innovations, but a digest of previous custom.

CHAPTER III.

HAMMURABI AND HIS REIGN

CONSIDERING the immense amount that has been written about Hammurabi during the last thirty years, it is remarkable how little is really known about him or his reign. The date when he lived is quite uncertain, the only approximation to it being derived from two inscriptions of the Babylonian monarch Nabonidus, who reigned from 555 to 538 B.C. This king rebuilt the Temple of the Sun at Sippara ; and in his foundation inscription he tells us that the edifice had previously been rebuilt by Shagashalti-Buriash, the son of Kudur-Bel, 800 years before ; that is to say, about 1350 B.C. Another inscription of Nabonidus informs us that Burna-Buriash, king of Babylon, rebuilt the great temple of Ur 700 years *after* Hammurabi. Burna-Buriash seems to have been an earlier monarch than Shagashalti-Buriash ; but there is nothing to show what distance of time separated them. Assuming that it was fifty

years (a very moderate estimate), then Hammurabi will have preceded Shagashalti-
Buriash by 750 years, and have flourished
about 2100 B.C. Most Assyriologists, however, consider this too late by at least a
century; and further particulars of the chronology of the period will be found in Appendix A.

Hammurabi was the sixth member of what
is called the "First Dynasty of Babylon."
Five of his ancestors bore Semitic Babylonian
names. His family had ruled in the city of
Babylon over a hundred years. It should,
therefore, be unnecessary to add that Hammurabi was undoubtedly a Semitic Babylonian
by race. The events of his reign are known
chiefly from the dates upon his contract
tablets. In those days people did not habitu-
ally date by any era; they did not even reckon
by the years of the king's reign. They
recorded each year by the principal event
which happened in it, whether it were an
inundation or a battle, or the building of a
temple or the excavation of a canal. Information from such sources is naturally limited in
its character. One event per annum tells us
very little about a monarch's reign; and for a
long time we were quite in the dark as to the

chronological order of the few events of which records existed. In 1891, however, Dr. Budge deposited in the British Museum a tablet he had acquired in the East, giving a list of the names of the years by which contracts were dated; and when this tablet was published by Dr. Pinches in 1898 scholars were at last able to construct something like a connected history of Hammurabi and his ancestors; although the tablet was badly damaged and only half legible.

Hammurabi's father, Sin-muballit, spent the greater part of his twenty-years' reign in peace, building city walls, digging canals, and decorating temples. But in his fourteenth year he defeated the army of the city of Ur; in his seventeenth year he stormed the city of Isin; and in his twentieth year he defeated the army of Larsam. He was then succeeded by his son, Hammurabi. We know very little of the first thirty years of the reign of Hammurabi. His first task appears to have been to tranquillise his dominions, for his second year is recorded on the contracts as being "the year in which Hammurabi established the heart of the land in righteousness."[1]

[1] *The Letters and Inscriptions of Hammurabi*, by L. W. King (London, 1900), vol. iii., p. 230.

For many subsequent years we have merely
fragmentary records of canals and build-
ings, etc.; but in his thirtieth year he
began the series of campaigns which made
him master of the *whole* of Babylonia ; for up
to this time he had only held the northern
half, and his ancestors had merely been rulers
of the city of Babylon and the surrounding
districts.

At the accession of Hammurabi Southern
Babylonia formed a separate State, of which
the capital was the city of Larsam.   Some
years previously the district had fallen under
the dominion of an Elamite, Kudur-Mabug,
the son of Simti-silkhak.   Kudur-Mabug did
not style himself " king," but only prince of
Emutbal and Martu (Emutbal was a border-
land between Babylonia and Elam, while
Martu was a name for Southern Babylonia).
His son and successor, however, called himself " Rim-Sin, the exalted shepherd of
Nippur, the preserver of Ur, king of Larsam,
king of Sumir and Akkad," and he reigned
at least thirty-seven years.[1]   We learn from
the tablet dates that he rebuilt the cities of

[1] " Die Datenliste der ersten Dynastie von Babylon," von
Ernest Lindl—*Beiträge zur Assyriologie*, band iv. (1901),
p. 382.

Nippur and Ur, which had evidently been partially ruined by war; he regulated part of the channel of the Euphrates and part of the channel of the Tigris. He founded (or rebuilt) the city of Kishurra, and destroyed Duran-ki (which is mentioned by Hammurabi in connection with Sippara). This clearly points to wars with the king of Babylon, probably Sin-muballit, in which Rim-Sin was occasionally successful. One of his dates reads "the year when Rim-Sin, the king, the goddess Nintu in the temple of the city of Kesh called *Te-an-ki-bi-da* 'the dominion of the world' abundantly and mightily elevated, and the wicked foe against the land did not fight." The *nakru limnu* or "wicked foe" appears again to be the king of Babylon. But the great event of the reign of Rim-Sin was the destruction of the city of Isin, which we have already seen was in the possession of Sin-muballit in his seventeenth year. We have tablets dated in "the year when, with the powerful aid of Anu Bel and Ea, the royal city of Isin was captured." Then "the year after the capture of Isin"; and so on up to "the thirtieth year after the capture of Isin." This city was an important one, and its rulers at one time reigned over

the greater part, if not the whole, of Babylonia. For thirty years, therefore, no action
of Rim-Sin's is recorded except the taking of
Isin.

In the thirtieth year of Hammurabi the
king of Babylon defeated an army of Elamites.
The next year the people of Southern Babylonia dated their contracts in "the year of
Hammurabi, the king, in which with the help
of Anu and Bel he established his good
fortune, and his hand cast to the earth the
land of Emutbal, and Rim-Sin, the king."
Evidently Anu and Bel had at last proved
false to Rim-Sin, and had transferred their
assistance to his adversary.

Two other royal names appear in connection with Larsam at this period. They are
Nur-Ramman and his son, Sin-iddinam. Of
the former we know nothing except that a
contract-tablet records an oath by "Nannar
and king Nur-Ramman"; there is nothing to
show if he were a temporary antagonist of
Rim-Sin or a vassal king set up by Hammurabi. Of Sin-iddinam we had a contract-
tablet dated in the year when the temple of
Eridu was finished and decorated with gold.
Also two inscriptions which recorded the
building of a couple of temples and the

construction of a canal.   But a few years ago the diggers in the mounds of Senkereh, which now cover the site of Larsam, came across a large collection of tablets, that are now preserved partly at Constantinople and partly at the British Museum, the latter collection having been published by Dr. L. W. King. These tablets comprised the letters which Sin-iddinam had received from Hammurabi. Evidently, after the overthrow of Rim-Sin, Hammurabi had set up Sin-iddinam as a vassal-king in Larsam ; and the correspondence indicates the complete subordination of the latter. Sin-iddinam's territory included Larsam, Ur, and several other cities; and his official title is given in one of the documents as *Gal Martu*—that is, "Governor of Martu."[1] This ought to settle the long controversy as to the exact locality of Martu, which is thus proved to be South-western Babylonia.

After a reign of forty-three years Hammurabi died, and left his dominions to his son Samsu-iluna.

Whatever more we may learn of his history in years to come, his greatest monument will ever be the Code of Laws which has been so

[1] King, *Letters of Hammurabi*, vol. iii., p. 169.

signally recovered at Susa. This Code must
have been promulgated late in his career, for
in the introduction to it he refers to Eridu,
Erech, Ur, Larsam, and other cities that did
not fall into his possession until his thirty-
first year; and in two passages of the prologue he alludes to his advanced age. The
extension of his territories had evidently forced
upon him the necessity of establishing a uni-
form system of law as the surest method of
organising and consolidating his kingdom;
and the next chapter will give a complete
translation of this remarkable inscription.

CHAPTER IV.

THE TEXT OF THE INSCRIPTION

WHEN Anu, the supreme, the king of the Anunnaki, and Bel, the lord of heaven and earth, who fixes the destiny of the universe, had allotted the multitudes of mankind to Merodach, the first-born of Ea, the divine master of Law, they made him great among the Igigi; they proclaimed his august name in Babylon, exalted in the lands, they established for him within it an eternal kingdom whose foundations, like heaven and earth shall endure.

Then Anu and Bel delighted the flesh of mankind by calling me, the renowned prince, the god-fearing Hammurabi, to establish justice in the earth, to destroy the base and the wicked, and to hold back the strong from oppressing the feeble: to shine like the Sun-god upon the black-haired men, and to illuminate the land.

Hammurabi, the elect shepherd of Bel, am I, dispenser of riches and abundance, completing all things in NIPPUR and Duran-ki, generous provider of *E Kur.*

The hero king who has restored ERIDU to its original state, purifier of the cult of *E Absu.*

Invader of the Four Quarters, exalter of the fame of BABYLON, rejoicer of the heart of his lord, Merodach, whom he daily serves in *E Saggil.*

The royal offspring created by Sin, who loads the city of UR with blessings, the humble suppliant who brings abundance to *E Nernugal.*

The prudent king, favoured of Shamash the powerful, the founder of SIPPARA, who has clothed with verdure the cenotaphs of Malkat; builder of *E Babbar* like heaven's throne.

Avenging warrior of LARSAM, restorer of *E Babbar* for the glory of Shamash, his helper.

The prince who has given life to ERECH by bringing abundant waters to its inhabitants, who has raised the head of *E Anna*, who has shaken out abundance over Anu and Nanna.

The protector of the land, who has reassembled the dispersed citizens of ISIN, who has made riches to abound in *E Galmakh.*

Guardian king of the city, brother of the

god Zamama, who has established the colony of KISH, who has enveloped *E Mete-ursag* with splendour. Decorator of the great sanctuaries of Nanna, sacristan of *E Kharsag-kalama.*

The grave of the foe, by whose help victory is attained, who has enlarged KUTHA, and amplified everything in *E Shidlam.*

The impetuous bull that overthrows the enemy, the darling of Tutu, the desire oɾ BORSIPPA; the august, the tireless for *E Zida.*

The divine urban king, the wise, the prudent, who has expanded the plantations of DILBAT, who has accumulated corn for Ninip, the mighty.

Possessor of sceptre and crown, whom the wise Mama has created, who has set out the boundary of KESH, who lavishes holy food for Nintu.

The far-seeing one, who has carefully provided pasture and drinking-places for SHIRPURLA and GIRSU, who has made rich offerings to *E L.*

The taker of enemies, the chosen of Telitim, accomplisher of the oracles of KHALLABI, who rejoices the heart of Anunit.

The pure prince whose prayers are heard by Adad, who contents the heart of Adad the warrior in KARKAR who has set out the vessels of *E Udgalgal.*

The king who has given life to ADAB, the prelate of the temple of *E Makh.*

The royal prince of the city, wrestler without rival, who has given life to MASHKAN-SHABRI, who has made [the temple of] *Shidlam* drink of abundance.

The wise, the active, who has struck down the bandits, who has sheltered the people of MALKA during troubles, and has established their habitations in abundance. Who has instituted pure offerings for ever for Ea and Damgalnunna, because they have exalted his sovereignty.

The royal ruler of the city who has subjugated the districts on the river Euphrates, the favoured of Dagan, his creator, who has rewarded the men of MERA and of TUTUL.

The renowned potentate, who has made the face of Nanna to shine, who has placed pure food before Ninazu, who fills his people during dearth, and assures them their goods in peace in the suburbs of BABYLON.

The shepherd of men, the servant who pleases Anunit, who installed Anunit in *E Ulmash* in the suburbs of AGADE.

The promulgator of justice, the guider of

the people, who has restored its tutelary deity to ASSUR.

The crusher of enemies, who has glorified the name of Nanna [Ishtar] in NINEVEH in *E Dupdup*.

The exalted one, who humbles himself before the great gods, the descendant of Sumula-ilu, the mighty son of Sin-muballit, the eternal scion of royalty, the powerful king, the sun of Babylon, beaming light over Sumir and Akkad, the king who is obeyed in the four quarters, the darling of Nanna am I.

When Merodach had instituted me governor of men, to conduct and to direct, Right and Justice I established in the land, for the good of the people.

1. If a man has laid a curse upon another man, and it is not justified, the layer of the curse shall be slain.

2. If a man has thrown a spell upon another man, and it is not justified, he who has suffered the spell shall proceed to the holy river: into the holy river shall he plunge. If the holy river seize him, the layer of the spell shall take his house. If the holy river holds him guiltless, and he

remains unharmed, the layer of the spell shall be slain. He that plunged into the holy river shall take the house of the layer of the spell.

3. If in a lawsuit a man gives damnatory evidence, and his word that he has spoken is not justified; then, if the suit be a capital one, that man shall be slain.

4. If he has offered corn or silver for evidence; then, whatever the penalty of that lawsuit, he shall suffer it.

5. If a judge has heard a case, and given a decision, and delivered a written verdict, and if afterwards his case be disproved, and that judge be convicted as the cause of the misjudgment; then shall he pay twelve times the penalty awarded in that case. In public assembly he shall be thrown from the seat of judgment; he shall not return; and he shall not sit with the judges upon a case.

6. If a man steal the goods of a god, or a palace, that man shall be slain. And whoever receives the booty at his hand shall be slain also.

7. If a man has bought silver, or gold, or man slave, or woman slave, or ox, or sheep, or ass, or anything else, from the hands of a child, or slave of another man, without elder

or contract, or receives them on deposit, that man shall be considered a thief: he shall be slain.

8. If a man has stolen an ox, or a sheep, or an ass, or a pig, or a boat, either from a god or a palace, he shall pay thirty-fold. If he is a plebeian, he shall render ten-fold. If the thief has nothing to pay, he shall be slain.

9. If a man has lost anything, and finds it in the hands of another; if the holder says, "A seller sold it me; before the elders I bought it." And if the claimant says, "I can produce witnesses who will recognise my property." Then the purchaser shall bring the vendor who gave it him, and the elders before whom he bought it; and the claimant the witnesses recognising his lost property. The judge shall weigh their evidence. The elders before whom the purchase was made, and the witnesses recognising the property, shall affirm before God what they know. The seller shall be held for a thief, and slain: the claimant shall receive back his lost property; and the purchaser shall receive back the money he paid from the house of the seller.

10. If the purchaser has not produced the seller from whom he received it, and the

elders before whom he bought it; but the claimant has brought witnesses recognising the property; then the purchaser shall be held for a thief, and slain; and the owner shall take his lost property.

11. If the claimant has not brought his witnesses recognising the property, he has acted in bad faith, he has calumniated; he shall be slain.

12. If the seller has gone to his fate, then from his house the purchaser shall claim five-fold as the penalty in the case.

13. If that man has not the elders at hand, the judge shall give him a time, up to six months. If in six months his witnesses do not appear, he has acted in bad faith; the penalty of that case he shall bear.

14. If a man has stolen a man's son under age, he shall be slain.

15. If a man has brought a male or female slave of the palace, or the male or female slave of a plebeian, to pass out of the gate, he shall be slain.

16. If a man has harboured in his house a fugitive male or female slave of the palace, or of a plebeian; and has not brought them to the order of the commandant, that house-holder shall be slain.

17. If a man has seized in the field a fugitive slave, male or female, and has brought him back to his lord, the owner of the slave shall pay him two shekels of silver.

18. If that slave will not name his owner, to the palace he shall be brought, his past shall be investigated, to his lord he shall be delivered.

19. If that slave be hidden in his house, and be arrested in his hands, that man shall be slain.

20. If a slave has escaped from the hand of his captor, the latter shall swear by the name of God to the owner of the slave, and shall be guiltless.

21. If a man has broken into a house, before the breach shall he be slain, and there buried.

22. If a man has perpetrated brigandage, and has been caught, that man shall be slain.

23. If the brigand has not been taken, the man plundered shall claim before God what he has lost; and the city and sheriff in whose land and boundary the theft has taken place shall restore to him all that he has lost.

24. If a life, the city and sheriff shall pay one mina of silver to his people.

25. If a fire break out in a man's house,

and another man has gone to extinguish it, and has lifted his eyes upon the goods of the householder, and has taken the goods of the householder; that man shall be thrown into the same fire.

26. If a captain or a soldier has been ordered upon "the way of the king," and has not gone, but has hired a substitute, that officer or soldier shall be slain. The substitute shall take his house.

27. If a captain or a soldier has been taken in "a misfortune of the king," and his field and garden have been given to another to administer; when he returns and regains his city, he shall receive back his field and garden and shall administer them.

28. If a captain or a soldier has been taken in "a misfortune of the king," and his son can work them; field and garden shall be given him, and the affairs of his father he shall administer.

29. If his son be under age, and unable to administer his father's affairs; then a third part of the field and garden shall be given to his mother, and his mother shall bring him up.

30. If a captain or a soldier has neglected his field, his garden, and his house, instead

of working them ; and another takes his field, his garden, and his house, and works them for three years ; if he returns and desires to till his field, his garden, and his house, they shall not be given him. He that has taken and worked them shall continue to use them.

31. If one year only he had neglected them, and he returns; field, garden, and house shall be restored to him, and he shall work them.

32. If a captain or a soldier has been taken prisoner on "the way of the king," and a merchant ransoms him, and brings him back to his city; then if his house contain sufficient for his ransom, he personally shall pay for his liberation. If his house do not contain sufficient, the temple of his city shall pay. If the temple of his city have not the means, the palace shall ransom him. His field, his garden, and his house shall not be given for his ransom.

33. If a prefect or a general permits evasion of service, and accepts a hired mercenary to go on "the way of the king," that prefect or general shall be slain.

34. If a prefect or a general has taken away the property of a captain, has injured a captain, has given a captain for hire, has abandoned the captain to a superior in a law-

D

suit, or taken away from the captain a gift of the king, that prefect or general shall be slain.

35. If any man purchase cattle or sheep that the king has given to a captain, he shall lose his money.

36. The field, garden, or house of a captain, or soldier, or vassal shall not be sold for silver.

37. If a man has bought the field, garden, or house of a captain, a soldier, or a vassal, his contract-tablet shall be broken, his money shall be forfeited, and the field, garden, or house shall be returned to the owner.

38. A captain, a soldier, or a vassal may not assign his field, or garden, or house to his wife or his daughter; neither can they be assigned for debt.

39. He may bequeath in writing to his wife or daughter a field, a garden, or a house that he may have bought, and may assign it for debt.

40. But he may sell his field, his garden, or his house to a merchant or another official; and the purchaser may work the field, garden, or house that he has bought.

41. If a man has enclosed the field, garden, or house of a captain, soldier, or vassal, and has provided the stakes; if the captain,

soldier, or vassal returns into the field, garden, or house, he shall pay for the stakes that have been provided.

42. If a man take a field to farm, and grows no corn on the field, he shall be accused of neglecting to work the field ; and he shall give to the lord of the field an amount of corn according to the yield of the district.

43. If he has not cultivated the field, but has let it lie fallow, he shall give corn like its neighbour to the lord of the field. And the field that lay fallow he shall hoe and sow, and to the lord of the field restore it.

44. If a man lease unreclaimed land for three years for cultivation, but has been lazy and has not worked the field; in the fourth year he shall break up the field, hoe it, and sow it, and to the lord of the field restore it. And he shall measure out to him ten *gur* of corn for each ten *gan*.

45. If a man has let his field to a cultivator for a rental, and has received the rental ; and if afterwards the god Adad [*i.e.,* a thunderstorm] has flooded the field and destroyed the harvest, the loss is to the cultivator.

46. If he has not received the rental of his field, or has let it for one-half or one-third of the crop; then the cultivator and the lord of

the field shall take their proportions of the corn that is left in the field.

47. If the cultivator, because he had made no profit in the preceding year, has sub-let the field for tillage, the lord of the field cannot condemn the cultivator. His field has been tilled, and at the harvest he shall take corn according to his contract.

48. If a man is liable for interest, and the god Adad has flooded his field, or the harvest has been destroyed, or the corn has not grown through lack of water; then in that year he shall not pay corn to his creditor. He shall dip his tablet in water, and the interest of that year he shall not pay.

49. If a man has received silver from a trader, and has given to the trader a cornfield or sesame-field, saying "I shall plant the field with corn or sesame; take and reap whatever there is," then when the cultivator has grown corn or sesame on the field, the lord of the field shall take corn or sesame, whatever is upon the field at the harvest; and shall give to the trader corn for the silver he has received from the trader, and for its interest; and sustenance for the cultivator.

50. If an already planted field, or a field already planted with sesame, has been given;

the lord of the field shall take the corn or sesame which is in the field, and he shall render silver and interest to the trader.

51. If he has not silver to pay back, he shall give to the trader sesame according to the value of the silver he has received, with its interest at the royal tariff.

52. If the cultivator has not grown corn or sesame in the field, his contract shall not be annulled.

53. If a man has been too lazy to strengthen his dyke, and has not strengthened the dyke, and a breach has opened in the dyke, and the ground has been flooded with water; the man in whose dyke the breach has opened shall reimburse the corn he has destroyed.

54. If he has not corn to reimburse, he and his goods shall be sold for silver, and it shall be divided among those whose corn has been destroyed.

55. If a man has opened his irrigation ditch, and, through negligence, his neighbour's field is flooded with water, he shall measure back corn according to the yield of the district.

56. If a man has opened the waters, and flooded the planted field of his neighbour, he shall measure back ten *gur* of corn for each ten *gan*.

57. If a shepherd has put his sheep to grass without an understanding with the lord of the field; and, unknown to the lord of the field, it has been grazed by the sheep; then the lord shall reap his fields, and the shepherd who has grazed his sheep unknown to the lord of the field shall pay to the latter in addition twenty *gur* of corn for every ten *gan*.

58. If, after the sheep have left the pasture, and been folded by the gate, a shepherd allows his sheep to remain in the field and graze; then that shepherd shall take that field which has been grazed, and at the harvest he shall measure sixty *gur* of corn for each ten *gan* to the lord of the field.

59. If a man, unknown to the lord of the orchard, has cut down a tree in another man's orchard, he shall pay half a mina of silver.

60. If a man has leased a field to a gardener to be converted into a garden, and the gardener has planted it; for four years he shall attend to it; in the fifth year the lord of the orchard and the gardener shall share equally. The lord of the orchard shall choose his share and take it.

61. If the gardener has not planted all the field, but leaves a waste, the waste shall be put in his portion.

62. If the field entrusted to him has not been planted as a garden, but is cornland; the gardener shall measure back to the lord of the field the produce of the field according to the yield of the vicinity during the years he has neglected it. And he shall prepare the field and return it to the lord.

63. If it is waste land, he shall prepare it, and restore it to the lord of the land, and he shall measure ten *gur* of corn per ten *gan* for each year.

64. If a man has leased an orchard to a gardener to cultivate it; the gardener, as long as he holds it, shall give two-thirds of the produce to the lord of the orchard, one-third he shall keep himself.

65. If the gardener has not cultivated the orchard, and the crop has diminished; the gardener shall measure out according to the yield of the vicinity.

[Five rows of cuneiform columns have here been erased. It is estimated that some thirty-five sections have thus been obliterated. The British Museum, however, possesses two fragments of clay tablets brought from the library of the Assyrian king Assurbanipal (reigned 668–626 B.C.) at Nineveh, which are the remains of copies of the Code. From these tablets the following three sections have been restored :—

a. If a man has received silver from a trader, and has pledged his date-garden to him, saying, " The dates in my garden take for thy silver," and the trader has not consented ; then the lord of the garden shall gather the dates which are in the garden : the silver and its interest according to the tenour of his tablet he shall pay to the trader ; and the remainder of the dates which are found in the garden shall be taken by the lord of the garden.

b. If a tenant has paid to the landlord his full rent for a year, and the landlord orders the tenant to go out before the days are completed, then because the tenant has not completed his days, and has left the house, the landlord shall return the silver which the tenant has paid him.

c. If a man owes corn or silver, but has neither corn nor silver to pay with, then shall he produce before the elders whatever property he has in his hands: to the trader he shall give it. The trader must accept it, and must not refuse.]

100. ......interest for the silver, as much as he has received, he shall write down ; and on the day when he makes account, he shall pay to his trader.

101. If in the place where he has gone he has found no opportunity, the retailer shall give back in equal amount to the trader.

102. If a trader has lent silver to a retailer for an undertaking, and where he has gone he has suffered loss, he shall return the capital sum to the trader.

103. If the enemy has taken from him whatever he carries upon the road, the retailer shall swear by the name of God, and shall be absolved.

104. If a trader has entrusted corn, wool, oil, or any other goods to a retailer to trade with, the retailer shall write down the price and give it to the trader. Thus shall the retailer take back the seal of the silver which shall be given to the trader.

105. If the retailer is negligent, and the seal of the silver has not been given to the trader, the silver that is not sealed shall not be carried to account.

106. If a retailer has received silver from a trader, and disputes with the trader; then the trader shall call the retailer before God and

the elders, regarding the silver received ; and the retailer shall restore three-fold the silver he has received.

107. If a trader has wronged a retailer, and the retailer has repaid to the trader all that the trader gave him, and the trader contests what has been given to him ; then that retailer shall call the trader before God and the elders; and because the trader has contested with his retailer, he shall pay to the retailer six-fold of all that he has received.

108. If a (female) wine-seller has not accepted corn as the price of drink, but silver by the grand weight has accepted, and the price of drink is below the price of corn ; then that wine-seller shall be prosecuted, and thrown into the water.

109. If rebels meet in the house of a wine-seller and she does not seize them and take them to the palace, that wine-seller shall be slain.

110. If a priestess who has not remained in the sacred building, shall open a wine-shop, or enter a wine-shop for drink, that woman shall be burned.

111. If a wine-seller has given sixty *qa* of *usakani* for refreshment, at the harvest she shall receive fifty *qa* of corn.

112. If a man goes on a journey and gives to another man silver, gold, gems, or ornaments of the hands, that they may be carried home, and that man has not carried and delivered all that was given him to carry, but has kept them; then the owner shall prosecute that man for all the things carried but not delivered, and that man shall pay five-fold to the owner for all that was given him.

113. If a man has a claim for corn or silver upon another man, and without the knowledge of the owner has taken corn from the granary or store; that man, because he has taken corn from the granary or store without the knowledge of the owner, shall be prosecuted. The corn he has taken shall be returned, and all that he should have received he shall lose.

114. If a man has no claim upon another man for corn or silver, but levies distraint upon him, for each distraint he shall pay one-third of a mina of silver.

115. If a man has a claim upon another man for corn or silver, and takes distraint, if the distrained die in the house of the distrainer by a natural death, then that case has no further claim.

116. If the distrained die in the house of

the distrainer through blows or ill-treatment, the distrainer shall call his trader to account. If he be freeborn, his son shall be slain ; if a slave, he shall pay a third of a mina of silver; and all that he should have received he shall lose.

117. If a man has contracted a debt, and has given his wife, his son, his daughter for silver or for labour, three years they shall serve in the house of their purchaser or bonds-master; in the fourth year they shall regain their original condition.

118. If he has assigned a male or female slave for labour, and the trader sends them out, and sells them for silver, there is no claim.

119. If a man has contracted a debt, and has sold for silver a slave who has borne him children; the lord of the slave shall pay back the silver the trader has given him, and the slave shall be free.

120. If a man has stored his corn in the granary of another man, and the store has been damaged, or the householder has opened the granary taking corn, or he disputes the quantity of the corn heaped up, then the owner of the corn shall pursue his corn before God, and the householder who has taken the corn shall replace it and give it to the owner.

121. If a man has stored corn in the house of another man, he shall pay five *qa* of corn per *gur* per annum for warehousing.

122. If a man desires to deposit with another man silver, gold, or anything else, he shall exhibit all before the elders, draw up a contract, and then make the deposit.

123. If he has given on deposit without elders or contract, and where he has given they contest it, there is no claim.

124. If a man has deposited silver or gold or anything else with another man before the elders, and if that man denies it, he shall prosecute him, and all that he contests he shall replace and restore.

125. If a man has given his goods on deposit, and in the place of deposit, either by breaking in or by climbing over, anything has been lost, together with property of the householder; then the householder in question shall make good all that was deposited with him and lost, and shall restore it to the owner. The householder shall pursue his stolen goods and recover from the thief.

126. If a man has not lost everything, but says everything of his is lost, exaggerating what is lacking; then, as he has not lost everything, his lack he shall bring before

God. All that he substantiates shall be made up; what he lacks shall be restored.

127. If a man has pointed the finger against a priestess or the wife of another man unjustifiably, that man shall be thrown before the judge, and his brow shall be branded.

128. If a man takes a wife, and a contract has not concluded, then that woman is no wife.

129. If the wife of a man is found lying with another male, they shall be bound and thrown into the water; unless the husband lets his wife live, and the king lets his servant live.

130. If a man has forced the wife of another man, who has not known the male, and who still resides in the house of her father, and has lain within her breasts, and he is found, that man shall be slain; that woman is guiltless.

131. If a man's wife has slandered her husband, but has not been found lying with another male, she shall swear by the name of God and return into her house.

132. If the finger is pointed against a man's wife because of another male, and she has not been found lying with another male; then she shall plunge for her husband into the holy river.

133. If a man has been taken prisoner, and there is food in his house, and his wife forsakes his house, and enters the house of another; then because that woman has not preserved her home, but has entered another house, then that woman shall be prosecuted, and shall be thrown into the water.

134. If a man has been taken prisoner, and there is no food in his house, and his wife enters the house of another; then that woman bears no blame.

135. If a man has been taken prisoner, and there is no food before her, and his wife has entered the house of another, and bears children, and afterwards her husband returns and regains his city; then that woman shall return to her spouse. The children shall follow their father.

136. If a man has abandoned his city, and absconded, and after that his wife has entered the house of another; if that man comes back and claims his wife; because he had fled and deserted his city, the wife of the deserter shall not return to her husband.

137. If a man has set his face to divorce a concubine who has borne him children, or a wife who has presented him with children; then he shall give back to that woman her

dowry, and he shall give her the usufruct of field, garden, and property, and she shall bring up her children.   After she has brought up her children, she shall take a son's portion of all that is given to her children, and she may marry the husband of her heart.

138. If a man divorce his spouse who has not borne him children, he shall give to her all the silver of the bride-price, and restore to her the dowry which she brought from the house of her father; and so he shall divorce her.

139. If there was no bride-price, he shall give her one mina of silver for the divorce.

140. If he is a plebeian, he shall give her one-third of a mina of silver.

141. If a man's wife, dwelling in a man's house, has set her face to leave, has been guilty of dissipation, has wasted her house, and has neglected her husband; then she shall be prosecuted.   If her husband says she is divorced, he shall let her go her way; he shall give her nothing for divorce.   If her husband says she is not divorced, her husband may espouse another woman, and that woman shall remain a slave in the house of her husband.

142. If a woman hate her husband, and

says "Thou shalt not possess me," the reason for her dislike shall be inquired into. If she is careful, and has no fault, but her husband takes himself away and neglects her; then that woman is not to blame. She shall take her dowry and go back to her father's house.

143. If she has not been careful, but runs out, wastes her house and neglects her husband; then that woman shall be thrown into the water.

144. If a man has married a wife and that wife has given to her husband a female slave who has children; then if that man has set his face to marry a concubine, he shall not be permitted; he shall not marry a concubine.

145. If a man has married a wife and she has not presented him with children, and he has set his face to marry a concubine; if that man marries a concubine and brings her into his house, then that concubine shall not rank with the wife.

146. If a man has married a wife, and she has given to her husband a female slave, who bears children; and afterwards that slave ranks herself with her mistress, because she has borne children, her mistress shall not sell her for silver. She shall be fettered, and counted among the slaves.

E

147. If she has not borne children, her mistress shall sell her for silver.

148. If a man has married a wife, and sickness has seized her, and he has set his face to marry another; he may marry; but his wife whom the sickness has seized he shall not divorce. She shall dwell in the house he has built, and he shall support her while she lives.

149. If that woman is not content to dwell in the house of her husband, he shall return to her the dowry she brought from her father's house, and she shall go.

150. If a man has given to his wife field, garden, house, or goods, and has given her a sealed tablet; then after her husband [has gone to his fate] her children have no claim. The mother can give what she leaves behind to the children she prefers. To brothers she shall not give.

151. If a woman who dwells in a man's house has bound her husband not to assign her to a creditor, and has received a tablet; then if that man had a debt upon him before he married that woman, his creditor may not seize his wife. And if that woman had incurred debt before she entered the man's house, her creditor may not seize her husband.

152. If, after that woman has entered the man's house, they incur debt, both of them must satisfy the trader.

153. If a man's wife, because of another male, has killed her husband, that woman shall be impaled upon a stake.

154. If a man has known his daughter, that man shall be banished from his city.

155. If a man has betrothed a bride to his son, and his son has known her ; and afterwards he has lain in her breasts, and he is found ; that man shall be bound and thrown into the water.

156. If a man has betrothed a bride to his son, and his son has not known her, and he has lain in her breasts, he shall pay half a mina of silver ; and all that she brought trom her father's house shall be returned to her, and she may marry the husband of her heart.

157. If a man after his father has lain in the breasts of his mother, both of them shall be burned.

158. If a man after his father is discovered in the breasts of his lady, who has borne children, that man shall be cut off from his father's house.

159. It a man has brought goods into the house of his father-in-law, and has given the

bride-price, and has looked upon another woman, and has said to his father-in-law, "Thy daughter I will not marry"; then the father of the girl shall retain all that has been brought.

160. If a man has brought goods into the house of the father-in-law, and has given the bride-price, and the father of the girl says "I will not give thee my daughter"; he shall equal all that has been brought him and repay it.

161. If a man has brought goods into the house of his father-in-law, and has given the bride-price, and his friend has slandered him, and the father-in-law has said to the husband of the wife, "My daughter thou shalt not marry"; he shall equal all that has been brought him and repay it; and his wife shall not marry his friend.

162. If a man has married a wife, and she has borne children, and that woman has gone to her fate; then her father has no claim upon her dowry. The dowry is her children's.

163. If a man has married a wife, and she has presented no children to him, and that woman has gone to her fate; if the bride-price which that man brought to the house of his father-in-law has been returned to him by his

father-in-law, then the husband has no claim upon that woman's dowry. The dowry is to her father's house.

164. If his father-in-law has not returned the bride-price in her dowry; then he shall deduct all her bride-price, and shall give back her dowry to her father's house.

165. If a man has made a gift of field, or garden, or house, to his son, the first in his eyes, and has sealed him a tablet; then, after the father has gone to his fate, when the brothers divide he shall retain the father's present which he has given him over and above the equal part that he shares in the possessions of his paternal house.

166. If a man has married wives to the children he has had, but has not married a wife to an infant son; then after the father has gone to his fate, when the brethren share the possessions of the paternal house, they shall give silver for a bride-price to their infant brother who has not married a wife, besides his share; and he shall be married to a wife.

167. If a man has married a wife, and she has borne him children, and that woman has gone to her fate; and after her he has married another woman who bears him children; then

after the father has gone to his fate, the children shall not share according to the mothers; but they shall take the dowries of their own mothers. The possessions of their paternal house they shall share equally.

168. If a man has set his face to disown his son, and has said to the judge, "I disown my son," then the judge shall look into his reasons. If the son has not borne a heavy crime which would justify his being disowned from filiation, then the father shall not disown his son from filiation.

169. If he has borne against his father a heavy crime justifying his being disowned from filiation; then for his first offence he shall turn aside his face. If he bear a heavy crime the second time, the father shall disown his son from filiation.

170. If a man whose spouse has borne him children, and whose female slave has borne him children, and the father in his lifetime has said to the children of the female slave "my children," and has counted them with the children of his spouse, and after that the father has gone to his fate; then the children of the spouse and the children of the female slave shall share the possessions of the paternal house equally. The sons that are

children of the wife shall choose and allot in the division.

171a. And if the father in his lifetime has not said to the children whom the female slave has borne him " my children," and afterwards the father has gone to his fate ; the children of the female slave shall not share with the children of the spouse ; but the slave and her children shall be emancipated, and the children of the spouse shall have no claim for service upon the children of the slave.

171b. The spouse shall take her dowry, and the settlement which her husband made her and wrote in a tablet for her, and she shall dwell in the domicile of her husband.   While she lives she shall enjoy it ; she may not sell it for silver, but after her it is her children's.

172a. If her husband has not made her a settlement, her dowry shall be returned to her, and she shall receive a portion of the possessions of her husband's house equal to that of a son.   If her children annoy her, to make her leave the house, the judge shall look into the reasons ; and, if the children be in fault, that woman shall not leave her husband's house.

172b. If that woman has set her face to depart, she shall surrender to her children the settlement which her husband made her. She shall retain the dowry from her father's house, and she may marry the husband of her heart.

173. If that woman where she has gone bears children to her later husband, and afterwards the woman dies; her former and her latter children shall share her dowry.

174. If she bears no children to her later husband, the children of her former consort take her dowry.

175. If either a palace slave, or the slave of a plebeian, marry the daughter of a free man, and she bears children; the owner of the slave has no claim for service upon the children of the free man's daughter.

176a. And if a palace slave or slave of a plebeian marry the daughter of a free man, and when she marries she enters the house of the palace slave or the plebeian's slave with a dowry from the house of her father; and when they are settled and have founded a house they have acquired property, and afterwards the palace slave or the slave of the plebeian has gone to his fate; then the daughter of the free man shall take her dowry; and all that her husband and herself have acquired since they settled shall be divided into two parts; the owner of the slave shall take half, and the free man's daughter shall take half for her children.

176b. If the free man's daughter had no dowry; all that her husband and herself have acquired since they settled shall be divided into two parts: the owner of the slave shall take half, and the free man's daughter shall take half for her children.

177. If a widow who has infant children has set her face to enter a second house, she shall not enter without [consent] of the judge. When she would enter the second house the judge shall inquire into the residue of her former husband's house. The house of her former husband and that woman shall be entrusted to the house of her later husband, and a tablet shall be delivered to them. They shall maintain the house and bring up the infants. They may sell nothing for silver. The purchaser who buys any vessel belonging to the widow's children shall lose his silver and the property shall return to its owner.

178. If a priestess, or a devotee, her father has given her a dowry, and has written a tablet; but has not written in the tablet that what she leaves behind her she may give as she sees good, and has not allowed the fulness

of her heart; and afterwards the father has gone to his fate; then her brothers shall take her field or her garden, and according to the value of her share they shall give her corn, oil, and wool, and her heart shall be satisfied. If her brothers have not given her corn, oil, and wool according to the value of her share, and her heart is not satisfied, then her field or her garden shall be entrusted to the cultivator whom she sees good, and her cultivator shall sustain her. While she lives she shall enjoy field and garden and everything which her father has given her; but she may not sell for silver nor alienate to another. Her filiation is to her brothers.

179. If a priestess or devotee her father has given her a dowry, and has written a deed, and has written in the tablet that what she leaves behind her she may give as she sees good, and has allowed the fulness of her heart; then after her father has gone to his fate she may give what she leaves behind to whom she sees good. Her brothers have no claim.

180. If the father has not given a dowry to his daughter who is a *Kallati* or a devotee; then after the father has gone to his fate, she shall take out of the possessions of the

paternal house the portion of one son. She shall enjoy it during her life. What she leaves behind is to her brothers.

181. If the father has consecrated a *Qadishtu* or a virgin to God, and has not given her a dowry ; after the father has gone to his fate she shall take out of the possessions of the paternal house one-third of the portion of a son. She shall enjoy it during her life. What she leaves behind is to her brothers.

182. If the father has not given a dowry to his daughter, a " wife of Merodach of Babylon " and not written a deed ; then after the father has gone to his fate she shall take out of the possessions of the paternal house one-third of the portion of a son with her brothers. She shall not have the management. The " wife of Merodach " may give what she leaves behind to whom she sees good.

183. If the father has provided a dowry for his daughter by a concubine, has found her a husband, and written her a deed ; then after the father has gone to his fate she shall not share in the possessions of the paternal house.

184. If the father has not provided a dowry for his daughter by a concubine, and has not found her a husband ; then after the father has

gone to his fate her brothers shall provide her a dowry according to the wealth of the paternal house and find her a husband.

185. If a man has taken an infant to adopt into his own name, and brought him up; that adopted son may not be reclaimed.

186. If a man has adopted an infant, and when he has taken him he injures his father and his mother; then that adopted son shall return to his father's house.

187. The son of a *Nersega*, an inmate of the palace, or the son of a devotee may not be reclaimed.

188. If a son of the people has taken a child to adoption, and has taught him his handicraft, he may not be reclaimed.

189. If he has not taught him his handicraft, that adopted son shall return to his father's house.

190. If a man has adopted an infant as a son, and brought him up, but has not reckoned him with his children; then that adopted son shall return to his father's house.

191. If a man has adopted an infant as a son, and brought him up, and has founded a household, and afterwards has had children, and if he has set his face to disown the adopted son; then that child shall not go his

way. His foster father shall give him out of his possessions one-third of the portion of a son, and then he shall go. Of field, or garden, or house, he shall not give him.

192. If the son of a *Nersega*, or the son of a devotee, to his foster father or his foster mother, has said, " Thou art not my father," or " Thou art not my mother "; his tongue shall be cut out.

193. If the son of a *Nersega*, or the son of a devotee, has come to know his father's house, and he despises his foster father and his foster mother, and goes to the house of his father; his eyes shall be torn out.

194. If a man has given his child to a nurse, and the child dies in the hand of the nurse, and the nurse without the knowledge of his father and his mother suckles another child; she shall be prosecuted, and because she has suckled another child without the knowledge of his father and his mother, her breasts shall be cut off.

195. If a son has struck his father, his hands shall be cut off.

196. If a man has destroyed the eye of a free man, his own eye shall be destroyed.

197. If he has broken the bone of a free man, his bone shall be broken.

198. If he has destroyed the eye of a plebeian, or broken a bone of a plebeian, he shall pay one mina of silver.

199. If he has destroyed the eye of a man's slave, or broken a bone of a man's slave, he shall pay half his value.

200. If a man has knocked out the teeth of a man of the same rank, his own teeth shall be knocked out.

201. If he has knocked out the teeth of a plebeian, he shall pay one-third of a mina of silver.

202. If a man strike the body of a man who is great above him, he shall publicly receive sixty lashes with a cowhide whip.

203. If a man strike the body of the son of a free man of like condition, he shall pay one mina of silver.

204. If a plebeian strike the body of a plebeian, he shall pay ten shekels af silver.

205. If a man's slave strike the body of the son of a free man, his ear shall be cut off.

206. If a man has struck another man in a dispute and wounded him, that man shall swear, "I did not strike him knowingly"; and he shall pay for the doctor.

207. If he die of his blows, he shall swear

likewise ; and if it be the son of a free man, he shall pay half a mina of silver.

208. If he be the son of a plebeian, he shall pay a third of a mina of silver.

209. If a man strike the daughter of a free man, and causes her fœtus to fall ; he shall pay ten shekels of silver for her fœtus.

210. If that woman die, his daughter shall be slain.

211. If he has caused the daughter of a plebeian to let her fœtus fall through blows, he shall pay five shekels of silver.

212. If that woman die, he shall pay half a mina of silver.

213. If he has struck the slave of a man, and made her fœtus fall ; he shall pay two shekels of silver.

214. If that slave die, he shall pay a third of a mina of silver.

215. If a doctor has treated a man with a metal knife for a severe wound, and has cured the man, or has opened a man's tumour with a metal knife, and cured a man's eye ; then he shall receive ten shekels of silver.

216. If the son of a plebeian, he shall receive five shekels of silver.

217. If a man's slave, the owner of the

slave shall give two shekels of silver to the doctor.

218. If a doctor has treated a man with a metal knife for a severe wound, and has caused the man to die, or has opened a man's tumour with a metal knife, and destroyed the man's eye; his hands shall be cut off.

219. If a doctor has treated the slave of a plebeian with a metal knife for a severe wound, and caused him to die; he shall render slave for slave.

220. If he has opened his tumour with a metal knife, and destroyed his eye, he shall pay half his price in silver.

221. If a doctor has healed a man's broken bone or has restored diseased flesh, the patient shall give the doctor five shekels of silver.

222. If he be the son of a plebeian, he shall give three shekels of silver.

223. If a man's slave, the owner of the slave shall give two shekels of silver to the doctor.

224. If a doctor of oxen or asses has treated either ox or ass for a severe wound, and cured it, the owner of the ox or ass shall give to the doctor one-sixth of a shekel of silver for his fee.

225. If he has treated an ox or an ass for a severe wound, and caused it to die, he shall

give the quarter of its price to the owner of the ox or the ass.

226. If a brander, unknown to the owner of a slave, has branded him with the mark of an inalienable slave, the hands of that brander shall be cut off.

227. If a man deceive a brander into branding with the mark of an inalienable slave, that man shall be slain and buried in his own house. The brander shall swear "I did not brand him with knowledge," and he shall be guiltless.

228. If a builder has built a house for a man, and completed it, he shall give him for his pay two shekels of silver for each *sar* [of surface] of the house.

229. If a builder has built a house for a man, and his work is not strong, and if the house he has built falls in and kills the householder, that builder shall be slain.

230. If the child of the householder be killed, the child of that builder shall be slain.

231. If the slave of the householder be killed, he shall give slave for slave to the householder.

232. If goods have been destroyed, he shall replace all that has been destroyed; and because the house that he built was not made

strong, and it has fallen in, he shall restore the fallen house out of his own personal property.

233. If a builder has built a house for a man, and his work is not done properly, and a wall shifts ; then that builder shall make that wall good with his own silver.

234. If a boat-builder has built a sixty-ton boat for a man, he shall give him two shekels of silver for his pay.

235. If a boat-builder has built a boat for a man and his work is not firm, and in that same year that boat is disabled in use ; then the boat-builder shall overhaul that boat, and strengthen it with his own material, and he shall return the strengthened boat to the boat-owner.

236. If a man has given his boat on hire to a boatman, and the boatman is careless, and the boat is sunk and lost ; then the boatman shall replace the boat to the boat-owner.

237. If a man has hired boatman and boat, and laden her with corn, wool, oil, dates, or any other kind of freight, and if that boatman is careless and sinks the boat, and her cargo is lost ; then the boatman shall replace the boat he has sunk and all her cargo that he has lost.

238. If a boatman has sunk a man's boat, and refloated her, he shall give silver to half her value.

239. If a man hire a boatman, he shall give him six *gur* of corn per annum.

240. If a *makhirtu* boat has run into a *mukkielbitu* boat and sunk her, the owner of the sunken boat shall pursue all that was lost in his boat before God. The *makhirtu* shall replace to the *mukkielbitu* boat that was sunk his boat and all that was lost in her.

241. If a man distrain an ox, he shall pay a third of a mina of silver.

242. If a man hires for a year, the fee for a draught ox is four *gur* of corn.

243. The fee for a milch-cow is three *gur* of corn given to the owner.

244. If a man has hired an ox or an ass, and a lion has killed it in the open country, then it is to the owner.

245. If a man has hired an ox, and by neglect or by blows has caused its death, he shall replace ox by ox to the owner of the ox.

246. If a man has hired an ox and broken its foot or cut the nape of its neck, he shall replace ox by ox to the owner of the ox.

247. If a man has hired an ox, and has

knocked out its eye, he shall give silver to the owner of the ox for half its value.

248. If a man has hired an ox, and has broken off its horn, or cut off its tail, or damaged its muzzle, he shall give silver for a quarter of its value.

249. If a man has hired an ox, and God has struck it, and it has died; then the man who hired the ox shall swear by the name of God, and shall be guiltless.

250. If a mad bull has rushed upon a man, and gored him, and killed him; that case has no remedy.

251. If a man's ox is known to be addicted to goring, and he has not blunted his horns, nor fastened up his ox; then if his ox has gored a free man and killed him, he shall give half a mina of silver.

252. If it be a man's slave, he shall give a third of a mina of silver.

253. If a man has let his field to another man to dwell upon its face, and has given him seed corn and entrusted him with draught oxen, and has contracted with him to cultivate the field; and if that man has stolen seed or plants, and they are found in his hands, his hands shall be cut off.

254. If he has received the seed, but

worn out the oxen, he shall replace by hoed corn.

255. If he has given the man's draught oxen on hire, or stolen the seed-corn and not grown it in the field, that man shall be prosecuted, and he shall measure out sixty *gur* of corn for every hundred *gan*.

256. If his prefect will not advance the compensation, he shall be placed with the cattle in the field.

257. If a man hire a field-labourer, he shall give him eight *gur* of corn per annum.

258. If a man hire a herdsman, he shall give him six *gur* of corn per annum.

259. If a man has stolen a water-wheel from the estate, he shall give five shekels of silver to the owner of the wheel.

260. If he has stolen an irrigating bucket or a harrow, he shall pay three shekels of silver.

261. If a man hire a pasturer for cattle and sheep, he shall give him eight *gur* of corn per annum.

262. If a man either ox or sheep...... [defaced].

263. If he has lost ox or sheep that has been entrusted to him, he shall replace ox by ox, sheep by sheep, to the owner.

264. If a herdsman who has had cattle or sheep given him to pasture, and has been paid his wages as agreed, and his heart is satisfied; and if the cattle he has made to diminish, or the sheep he has made to diminish, and has made the progeny to decline; then he shall give progeny and number according to his agreement.

265. If a herdsman to whom cattle and sheep have been given to pasture has lied, and has altered the bargain, and sold for silver; then he shall be prosecuted. He shall restore cattle or sheep to their owner tenfold what he has stolen.

266. If a stroke of God has occurred in a fold, or a lion has slain, then the herdsman shall clear himself before God, and the owner of the fold shall meet the disaster to the fold.

267. If the herdsman is in fault, and has been the occasion of the loss in the fold; then the herdsman shall restore the cattle and sheep which he has caused to be lost in the fold, and shall give them back to the owner.

268. If a man has hired an ox for threshing, twenty *qa* of corn is its hire.

269. If an ass has been hired for threshing, ten *qa* of corn is its hire.

270. If a young animal has been hired for threshing, one *qa* of corn is its hire.

271. If a man hire cattle, wagon, and driver, he shall give 180 *qa* of corn per diem.

272. If a man has hired a wagon by itself, he shall give forty *qa* of corn per diem.

273. If a man hire a workman, then from the beginning of the year until the fifth month he shall give six grains of silver per diem. From the sixth month until the end of the year he shall give five grains of silver per diem.

274. If a man hire a son of the people,

(*a*) Pay of a	five grains of silver,
(*b*) Pay of a potter	five grains of silver,
(*c*) Pay of a tailor	five grains of silver,
(*d*) Pay of a mason	...... grains of silver,
(*e*) Pay of a	.... of silver,
(*f*) Pay of a	.... of silver,
(*g*) Pay of a carpenter	four grains of silver,
(*h*) Pay of a ropemaker	four grains of silver,
(*i*) Pay of a	...... grains of silver,
(*j*) Pay of a builder	...... grains of silver,

he shall give per diem.

275. If a man hire a ......, her hire is three grains of silver per diem.

276. If a man hire a *makhirtu*, he shall give two and a half grains of silver per diem for her hire.

277. If a man hire a sixty-ton boat, he shall give a sixth part of a shekel of silver per diem for her hire.

278. If a man has bought a slave, male or female, and before his month has expired the *bennu* sickness has fallen upon him ; then he shall return him to the vendor, and the buyer shall receive back the purchase money.

279. If a man has bought a slave, male or female, and there is a claim, then the vendor shall answer the claim.

280. If a man has bought another man's slave, male or female, in a foreign land, and when he has come into the midst of the country the master of the slave recognises his male or female slave; then, if they are children of the land, they shall receive their freedom without price.

281. If they are children of another land, the purchaser shall take oath before God as to the silver he has paid ; and the owner of the slave, male or female, shall give to the trader the silver he has paid ; and shall recover his male or his female slave.

282. If a slave shall say to his master, "Thou art not my master," he shall be prosecuted as a slave, and his owner shall cut off his ear.

The judgments of justice which Hammurabi, the mighty king, has established, conferring upon the land a sure guidance and a gracious rule.

Hammurabi, the protecting king, am I. I have not withdrawn myself from the black-headed race that Bel has entrusted to me, and over whom Merodach has made me shepherd. I have not reposed myself upon my side ; but I have given them places of peace. Difficult points have I made smooth, and radiance have I shed abroad. With the mighty weapon that Zamama and Ishtar have lent me ; with the penetration with which Ea has endowed me ; with the valour that Merodach has given me, I have rooted out all enemies above and below ; and the depths have I subjugated. The flesh of the land I have made rejoice : the resident people I have made secure ; I have not suffered them to be afraid. It is I that the great gods have elected to be the Shepherd of Salvation, whose sceptre is just. I throw my good shadow over my city. Upon my bosom I cherish the men of the lands of Sumir and Akkad. By my protecting genius, their brethren in peace are guided : by my wisdom are they sheltered. That the strong may not oppress the weak ; that the orphan and the widow may be counselled ; in Babylon, the city whose head has been lifted up by Anu and Bel ; in E Saggil, the temple whose foundations are as solid as heaven and earth : to proclaim the law of the land : to guide the procedure of the land : and to sustain the feeble ; I have written my precious words upon my pillar, and before my image as King of Justice I have placed it.

I am the monarch who towers above the kings of the cities. My words are well weighed ; my valour has no equal. By command of Shamash, the great judge of heaven and earth, justice shall glisten in the land. By direction of Merodach, my lord, my monument shall never see destruction. In E Saggil that I love, my name shall ever be spoken. The oppressed, who has a law-suit, shall come before my image as king of justice. He shall read the writing on my pillar, he shall perceive my precious words. The word of my pillar shall explain to him his cause, and he shall find his right. His heart shall be glad [and he shall say] " The Lord Hammurabi has risen up as a true father to his people ; the will of Merodach, his god, he has made to be feared ; he has achieved victory for Merodach above and below. He has rejoiced the heart of Merodach, his lord ; and gladdened the flesh of his people for ever. And the land he has placed in order." Reading the mandates he shall pray before my lord Merodach and my lady Zarpanit with a full heart, and the guardian spirits, the deities, who reside in E Saggil within E Saggil, shall daily intercede before Merodach my lord, and Zarpanit my lady.

In after days and for all time, the king who is in the land shall observe the words of justice which are written upon my pillar. He shall not alter the law of the land which I have formulated, or the statutes of the country that I have enacted : nor shall he damage my sculptures. If that man has wisdom, and desires to keep his land in order, he will heed the words which are written upon my pillar. The canon, the rule, the law of the country which I have formulated, the statutes of the country that I have enacted, this pillar shall show to him. The black-headed people he shall govern ; their laws he shall pronounce, their statutes he shall decide. He shall root out of the land the perverse and the wicked ; and the flesh of his people he shall delight.

Hammurabi, the king of justice, am I, to whom Shamash has granted rectitude. My words are well weighed : my deeds have no equal, levelling the exalted, humbling the proud, expelling the haughty. If that man heeds my words that I have engraved upon my pillar, departs not from the laws, alters not my words, changes not my sculptures, then may Shamash make the sceptre of that man to endure as long as I, the king of justice, and to lead his people with justice.

But if that man heeds not my words that I have written upon my pillar ; if he has scorned my malediction, nor feared the curse of God ; if he has annulled the law that I have given, or altered my words, or changed my sculptures, or erased my name in order to write his own. Or if, from fear of these curses, he has commissioned another ; then that man, whether he be king, or prince, or feudatory, or citizen, whatever his title, may the great Anu, the father of the gods, who has decreed my reign, may he extinguish the splendour of his royalty, may he shatter his sceptre, may he curse his end.

May the lord Bel, who fixes fate, whose word is inalterable, and who has magnified my royalty ; may he allot him a rebellion which his hand cannot quell : the breath of his ruin may he breathe upon his throne :

years of sighing : fewness of days : years of famine : darkness without light : and a death with open eyes. May his deep mouth decree him the overthrow of his city, the dispersion of his people, the removal of his royalty, and the annihilation of his name and memory in the land.

May Beltis, the great mother, whose word is great in E Kur, the lady who gives ear to my desires in the place of justice and statutes before Bel ; may she make his cause bad before Bel ; may she put in the mouth of Bel, the king, to devastate his land, to annihilate his people, and to pour out his soul like water.

May Ea, the great prince, whose decisions take first place, the divine thinker, the omniscient, who has lengthened the days of my life; may he take understanding and prudence from him ; may he plunge him in forgetfulness, obstruct his rivers at their sources, and prevent the growth of corn, the life of men, in his land.

May Shamash, the great judge of heaven and earth, who maintains all living creatures, the lord who gives confidence ; may he cut short his kingship, misjudge his law, obstruct his path, arrest the march of his troops, give him unpropitious visions of the uprooting of the foundation of his rule, and the ruin of his land. May the decree of Shamash hasten after him ; may he lack life on earth ; may he lack water among the spirits under the earth.

May Sin, the lord of the heavens, the divine creator, whose crescent shines among the gods ; may he take from him diadem and throne of royalty ; may he lay heavy sin upon him, with a penalty which shall never depart out of his body; may he complete the days of the months, the months of the years of his reign in sighs and tears ; may the cares of government be multiplied to him ; may he destine him a life which is a struggle with death.

May Adad, the lord of fertility, the prince of the heavens and the earth, my helper ; may he take away from him the rains of heaven, and dry up the outflow of springs ; may he waste his territory with want and famine ; may he thunder his anger against his city ; may he turn his dominions into ruins by tempests.

May Zamama, the great warrior, the eldest son of E Kur, who marches at my right hand upon the field of battle ; may he break his weapons ; may he convert his day into night, and cause his foe to triumph over him.

May Ishtar, the mistress of battles and combats, who wields my weapons, my guardian angel, who loves my reign; may she in her passionate heart, in her deep anger curse his royalty, turning her favours into evils; may she shatter his weapons upon the field of battles and combats; may she bring tumult and rebellion upon him; may she overthrow his warriors, soaking the earth with their blood; may she strew the corpses of his armies in heaps over the plain, giving them no quarter; may he be delivered into the hand of his foes, a prisoner in the enemy's land.

May Nergal, the mighty among the gods, whose onslaught none can withstand, who has granted me victory; with his mighty force may he burn up his people like a wisp of rushes; with his powerful weapons may he lop off his limbs, and shatter him like an image of clay.

May Nintu, the sublime lady of the lands, the creative mother; may she deny him offspring, and leave him no name, and create no seed of mankind in the habitations of his people.

May Nin-Karrak, the daughter of Anu, the herald of my mercy in E Kur; may she let loose in his members a violent sickness, a noisome pestilence, a fearsome wound which cannot be cured, whose nature no doctor can tell, that cannot be assuaged by bandage, which—like the bite of death—cannot be avoided, until she conquer his life ; and over the loss of his vigour he shall groan.

May the great gods of heaven and earth, the Anunnaki in their totality, the circuit of this temple of E Babbara ; may they all curse him with deadly curses, his reign, his land, his officers, his people, and his soldiers.

May Bel, whose word is irrevocable, may he curse him with a mighty curse, which shall immediately take effect.

CHAPTER V.

NOTES ON THE CODE

IN order to avoid breaking up the text of the inscription with notes, all remarks upon it are relegated to this chapter; and, as it may be useful to compare the Babylonian Laws with another Code that is undoubtedly independent of them, occasional references are made to the early Roman legislation called the Laws of the Twelve Tables. It is true that the *XII Tabulæ* were not formulated until 450 B.C.; but, as geographical and historical considerations render nugatory all suggestions of Babylonian influence, there can be no doubt of their entire independence. The Rome of the Decemvirs was in a more barbarous stage than the Babylon of Hammurabi; hence the laws were in many cases more crude; but we may at least recognise that very similar problems confronted the jurists of Italy and of Babylonia.

First of all, perhaps, attention should be directed to the bas-relief upon the top of the pillar. This represents Hammurabi adoring Shamash, the Sun-god. We know it is Shamash by the Cultus-tablet of Sippara, dedicated by Nabupaliddina about 870 B.C., which bears the same figure.[1] We know the king is in the attitude of adoration from the same sculpture, and from the innumerable seal-cylinders with similar subjects. Several commentators have said that Hammurabi's pillar represents the king as receiving his laws from Shamash; but such statements are in direct conflict with the inscription, which consistently claims that the laws were originated by Hammurabi himself. The epilogue commences with the words, *Dinât misharim sha Hammurabi sharrum lium ukinnuma*—" The judgments of justice which Hammurabi, the mighty king, has established " (*verso* xxiv. 1–5). Later on it makes Hammurabi speak of the law of the land which he has formulated, and the statutes of the country that he has enacted (xxv. 64–83), and it is impossible to make him claim the authorship of the Code in stronger language. It is true that he refers several times to the god Shamash, " the great judge of heaven and earth," as the

---

[1] *Babylonian Religion and Mythology*, by L. W. King (London, 1899), p. 19.

source and the supporter of law and justice; but that is quite another thing to claiming that the Code was dictated by the Sun-god.

Shamash is represented upon the bas-relief seated upon a throne, with his feet resting upon the rows of cones which, in Babylonian art, represent rocks or mountains; and one of the names of the Sun-god was *Il Shadde*, or "god of mountains," which has been compared with the Hebrew *El Shaddai*. The deity is draped in the usual flounced dress: from his shoulders rise wavy lines—intended to symbolise rays of light; and on his head he wears a lofty four-horned tiara. In his right hand he holds an object that looks like the cheek of a snaffle-bit, but which is best explained as a ring and a stylus. The ring symbolises the circle of the year; the stylus is the implement of the recording judge; because, as in most mythologies, the sun is the god of justice. The consort of Shamash was *Malkat*, "princess"; and his two sons were *Kettu*, "Law," and *Mesharu*, "Justice." The Sun-god was a favourite subject upon the ancient Babylonian seal-cylinders, where he is often represented as rising up from the Mountains of the East, while the attendant genii throw

open the doors of the Dawn before him.[1]   On
a remarkable cylinder illustrated by Dr.
Delitzsch[2] we have Shamash seated, with all
his attributes, upon a curious boat whose two
ends taper off into human forms, this boat
being the craft which takes the god across the
waters of the under-world during the night in
order that he may rise from the eastern
horizon in the morning.

Underneath the bas-relief the inscription
commences with the words *Ninu Anu Çirum*,
" When Anu the supreme "; and, in accordance with Babylonian custom, these three
words became in later times the title, or
heading, of the whole code ;[3] for, as we have
already remarked, the Code of Hammurabi
was the authoritative law-book of Babylonia
down to the latest period, and it existed in the
cuneiform libraries as a series of fifteen clay
tablets bearing the above title.   The second
word is simply written with the cuneiform sign
AN, which stands indifferently for the name
of the god "Anu," and the word *ilu*, "god."
As, however, the sign frequently figures

[1] King, *Babylonian Religion*, p. 32.

[2] *Babel and Bible*, translated by C. H. W. Johns, M.A.
(London, 1903), p. 74, fig. 49.

[3] *Proc. Soc. Bib. Arch.*, vol. xxiv., p. 304.

alone upon the contracts of the period as
the name of Anu, we are justified in accepting
it as bearing this reading in the inscription.
As, moreover, the next phrase contains the
special title of Anu, "king of the Anunnaki"
(or spirits of the heavens), it is immaterial
whether we render "When the supreme God,
the king of the Anunnaki," or, "When Anu,
the supreme, the king of the Anunnaki"; for
the phrases would be of identical mythological import.

The *Igigi* were the heavenly gods.

The "black-haired men" were the inhabitants of Babylonia, the phrase going back to
Akkadian times.

In the list of places which follows we have
put the names of the cities in small capital
letters, for more easy reference. Each city is
accompanied with the title of its chief temple,
which we have put in italic type. The temple
may also be recognised by the prefix *E*, an old
Akkadian word meaning "house" (Semitic
Babylonian *bit*, the Hebr e בֵּת, *beth*). Thus
E Kur is "the house of the land"; *E Absu*
"the house of the abyss," etc.

In SIPPARA the chief temple was *E Babbar*,
"the house of light," dedicated to Shamash.
His consort Malkat (in Akkadian *Aa*) was the

Persephone of the Babylonian pantheon, and it appears that her grave was shown in the temple covered with green turf, for she represented Nature in her winter sleep from which she is revived by the summer sun. Consequently, her symbol in the great temple of Sippara was the "verdant cenotaph" restored by the pious care of Hammurabi.

The city of ISIN had been destroyed by Rim-Sin; and lay in ruins for thirty years, until Hammurabi made himself master of southern Babylonia and resettled the city with its old inhabitants.

Nergal, the god of the dead, was the tutelary deity of KUTHA, which, accordingly, was the centre of an enormous cemetery. Therefore, Hammurabi appropriately styles himself "the *grave* of the foe" when he refers to this city and its temple.

The chief temple of SHIRPURLA[1] was denoted by the two characters E and 50. It is the usual practice of Assyriologists to transcribe the Babylonian numerals by the Roman, to which they bear great analogy. Thus *E L* would be the "house of the Fifty," or the "house of the god Fifty"—*i.e.*, Bel.

---

[1] GIRSU was merely the sacred quarter of the city. See *Records of the Past*, New Series, vol. i., p. 47.

KHALLABI was the Semitic name of an important city of Southern Babylonia called *Zariunu* in Akkadian. It stood in the vicinity of Sippara. The British Museum has a tablet of Rim-Sin recording the erection of a temple to the goddess of this city, and also another tablet recording that Hammurabi rebuilt the same temple.[1] Evidently the edifice was commenced by the one and finished by the other.

It is interesting to note the name of NINEVEH at the end of the list, for this is the first known mention of the city that afterwards became so celebrated as the capital of the realm of Assyria, which took its name from ASSUR, the cradle of the Assyrian power.

Hammurabi's list of cities is enough to prove that his was not a world-empire. His kingdom extended from Nineveh to the Persian Gulf, and embraced a territory slightly larger than Italy. Most of the places named are well known in early Babylonian history, some of them being at one time the centres of independent States. The mention of Nippur, Ur, and Larsam is noteworthy, for this shows that the inscription is later than the conquest

[1] King, *Letters of Hammurabi*, iii., p. 185.

of southern Babylonia. That is to say, it
cannot have been set up before Hammurabi's
thirty-first year. The king lived for twelve
years after his overthrow of Rim-Sin, and the
Code must have been formulated in the
interval.

THE THREE ESTATES OF BABYLONIA.

Before considering the individual precepts
it will be necessary to say something regarding the three classes of people presupposed
by the Code. We have, first, the slave;
secondly, the free man; thirdly, the MASH-EN-
KAK. The status of slavery offers no particular difficulty, and the provisions regarding it
can be easily understood. The status of free
man is less decisive. Most of the sections
begin with the words *shumma amelu*, "If a
man"; and in most cases the *amelu* must be a
man of any degree. But, *e.g.*, § 207, *mar
ameli*, can only mean "son of a *free* man";
and § 209, *marat ameli*, "daughter of a *free*
man," because there are other penalties for
the sons and daughters of other classes of
society. The context is practically our only
guide in determining when *amelu* means a
man in general, and when it is limited to a
free man, or full citizen.

The real difficulty of the Code lies in the third class. All through the Code we have definite regulations regarding a MASH-EN-KAK. Father Scheil gives this provisional reading to the three characters, and compares it with the Hebrew מסכן, adopted into the Italian as *meschino;* and thus into the French *mesquin,* " mean " or " shabby." The Mash-enkak, however, was by no means a pauper. He possessed silver, § 140; and he owned slaves, Sections 15, 175, 219; and his slaves were sometimes sufficiently well-off to marry free women, Sections 175, 176. A mere artisan, or man who lives by his labour, is not a Mashenkak; he is styled a *mar ummia,* or " son of the people," Sections 188, 274; and the " son of the people " was evidently a free man, like the other persons who served for wages and are mentioned in Sections 239, 257, 258, 261, and 271. A slave could be emancipated; but there is nothing in the Code to show how a Mashenkak could change his condition. His status depended upon birth, for Sections 208, 216, 222 deal with the *son* of a Mashenkak, and § 211 to a *daughter* of the same. The Mashenkak's life and limb were valued at less than those of a free man, and more than those of a slave, Sections 198,

201, 204. Consequently, he stood midway between the class of full freeman and the class of full slave, and the term "plebeian" would seem to best express his condition. When § 15 wishes to express the idea of "the slave of a man of high degree, or the slave of a man of low degree," it uses the terms, "slave of the palace or slave of a plebeian"; therefore, the plebeian was the humblest individual who could be thought of as possessing slaves.

SEMITIC IDIOMS.

The translation of the Code has been made as literally as possible consistent with intelligibility; hence idiomatic expressions are left as in the original. These need not offer any difficulty, for some are familiar from the Old Testament and the others are easily comprehensible. The following are a few examples :—

§ 137. "Set his face" = has a design to.

§ 169. "Turn aside his face" = change his intention.

§ 162. "Gone to her fate" = has died. *Shimtu* means "fate," or "destiny," or "lot"; and, as death is the common lot of humanity, the Babylonian idiom expressed it as going to one's destiny.

§ 137. "The husband of her heart"—*i.e.*, of her own choice.

§ 194. " In the hand of " = in the possession of ; etc.

OF SORCERY.

The Babylonians distinguished two kinds of witchcraft—viz., *nertu* and *kispu,* which we have here translated by " curse " and "spell." A man who considered himself bewitched would resort to the village *Asu.* The Asu (translated in this Code by "doctor") combined in himself the offices of exorcist, medicine man, physician, and surgeon. His method of procedure was usually to pronounce a counter-spell upon the suspected wizard. Such a suspicion, however, might be without foundation, and a perfectly innocent man might find himself in the unpleasant predicament of being denounced before his neighbours as a wizard, and himself the subject of the village magician's exorcism, carrying with it unknown perils to the superstitious mind. The Code, therefore, gives the suspected party the right of challenging the exorcism ; and we know from African examples that a native will face any ordeal to clear himself from the suspicion of witchcraft. The Code does not inform us how *nertu* was to be justified—perhaps that could be made the subject of judicial inquiry; but the sufferer from *kispu* could claim the ordeal by water, and the "River-God"[1] decided the case. Not only did the Babylonians consider sorcery an actual thing capable of being dealt with legally, but the Romans, who are usually considered a practical, hard-headed people, were fully convinced of the reality of magic, and the XII. Tables (viii. 8) forbid a man to remove his neighbour's crops from one field to another by incantation, or to conjure away his corn.

§ 4. Silver and corn formed the customary currencies of Babylonia. The silver was in the form of bullion, for coined money was not introduced until the reign of the Persian king, Darius Hystaspes. The table of weight was as follows :—

180 grains	=	1 shekel
60 shekels	=	1 mina
60 minæ	=	1 talent

(The Babylonian grain was somewhat heavier than the English.)

---

[1] In the inscription the word for "river" has the sign for divinity prefixed to it.

The corn measure ran :—

$$60 \text{ gin} = 1 \text{ qa}$$
$$300 \text{ qa} = 1 \text{ gur}$$

No certain English equivalents of these weights and measures can be given. See notes on § 42 and § 234.

§ 5. The XII. Tabb. (ix.) directed the execution of any judge convicted of taking a bribe. The Babylonian goes further, and degrades the judge who gives an unjust verdict, though there is no question of bribery.

§ 6 only speaks of the goods of god or palace ; but it appears from the context of Sections 7, 9, 10 that the theft of private property was visited with the same penalty. The "goods of a god" are, of course, the temple property. Throughout the Code we find the word *ilu*, "god," used indefinitely, as "a god." Such a practice no more implies that the Babylonians were monotheists than such names as Theodorus or Theophilus prove the ancient Greeks to have been monotheists. The "palace" is *Ekal* in the original, and the *Ekal* is not necessarily the residence of the king. In one of Hammurabi's letters, for example,[1] a revenue official speaks of the "palace" as the recipient of the

[1] King, *Letters of Hammurabi*, iii., p. 49.

local taxes. Consequently, the *Ekal* must be the residence of the governor of the locality. In § 176 "slave of the palace" is first mentioned, and then "the owner of the slave," so that it is not an edifice, but a person, that the legislator has in view.

§ 8. A *boat* is reckoned as a living thing, and is mentioned together with animals. The Roman Law of theft in the XII. Tabb. (viii. 16) limited the penalty to double the value of the property stolen; but if the thief were taken in the act, and found to be a free man, he was scourged and sold into slavery; if already a slave, he was hurled from the Tarpeian rock.

§ 9 shows the importance attached to written documents.

§ 21. The XII. Tabb. (viii. 12, 13) prescribe that a thief may lawfully be killed if taken in the act at night; but not by day, unless he be armed and resists capture.

§ 24. The locality had to pay blood-money to the relatives of a murdered man if the murderer could not be found. This clause and § 153 are the only places where murder is mentioned in the Code.

§ 25. The XII. Tables (viii. 10) directed that if a man set fire to a house, or a stack of corn near a house, the incendiary was to be bound, scourged, and burned alive.

OF MILITARY SERVICE.

The Babylonian kings (and also the Assyrians) provided themselves with soldiers by a kind of feudal system. Portions of the royal domains were allotted to individuals, who were bound to serve in the army when called upon. A vassal summoned on "the way of the king" was executed as a deserter if he did not appear. The phrase "way of the king," as Dr. Winckler[1] remarks, reminds us of the Arabic "Way of Allah," meaning a campaign. In Islam, Allah has taken the place of the king as director of the war. A defeat of the Babylonian army is euphemistically styled "a misfortune of the king."

§ 32 shows that the temple played a part in the village organisation similar to that of a medieval parish church. The soldier who could not pay his own ransom could claim it from his local temple. But if from poverty, or invasion, or the number of similar claims, the temple was unable to provide the money, then only did "the palace" intervene as a last resort.

[1] *Die Gesetze Hammurabis,* von Dr. H. Winckler (Leipsic, 1903), p. 13. n. 1.

§ 42. Three *gur* of corn was reckoned an average yield for a *gan* of land; and the yearly rent of a *gan* was usually one *gur* of corn. Our knowledge of Babylonian metrology, however, is not sufficient to enable exact equivalents of these measures to be given;[1] but the proportions stated will enable one to gauge roughly the onerousness of the various penalties set down in the Code.

§ 45. The Babylonians looked upon most of the operations of nature as due to the direct interference of the gods; thus Sections 45, 48, speak of the god Adad as flooding the fields. Adad was the deity of storms and thunder; hence in this place his name is to be read as the equivalent of "thunderstorm." There is a similar expression, "stroke of God," in § 266.

§ 48. The dipping of the tablet in water was a symbolical act.

§§ 57, 58. The XII. Tabb. (viii. 6, 7) prescribe that a quadruped that has damaged a neighbour's land shall be given to the aggrieved party, unless the owner make compensation. And he that pastures his animals on a neighbour's land is liable to an action.

§ 59. XII. Tabb. (viii. 11). "If a man

[1] *Assyrian Deeds and Documents*, by Rev. C. H. W. Johns (Cambridge, 1901), vol. ii., cap. iii.

wrongly fell his neighbour's trees, he shall pay a penalty of twenty-five *ases* of bronze in respect of each tree."

THE ERASURE UPON THE PILLAR.

After § 65 comes the erasure already mentioned. In the Kouyunjik collection of the British Museum, however, there is a tablet, No. R.M. 277, which contains in its first column of writing a complete copy of § 58 of the Hammurabi Code, preceded by a fragment of § 57, and followed by the commencement of § 59. In the second column of this tablet is another law which we have transcribed as § *a*. The reverse of this same tablet, although very much mutilated, exhibits detached fragments of Hammurabi's Sections 107, 113, 114, 115, 119, and 120. There can thus be no doubt that the intermediate paragraph (*a*) belonged to the now obliterated portion of the Code.

Another British Museum tablet, No. D.T. 81, bears on its face the law we have transcribed as § *b*, and on its reverse § *c*, together with fragments of Sections 103, 104, 111, and 112. So that here again it is clear that we have another copy of the Code which has preserved to us obliterated parts of the pillar.

H

If these two tablets were in good condition, they would have given us the whole of the missing ordinances ; but, unfortunately, they are both badly mutilated.

§ 100. When the column again becomes legible, it is found to be dealing with trading affairs. The Babylonian principal (*Tamkar*, "trader") stayed at home and looked after his warehouses and accounts. Agents, or pedlars, were entrusted with the duty of travelling about the country and making sales or purchases. The agent (*Shagan-lal*) we translate as " retailer."

§ 108. The Babylonian wine was prepared from dates, as the grape-vine is not indigenous to the country. The term " wine-seller " is preceded by the determinative for " woman," so that the wine-seller was evidently a female. The Assyrians and Babylonians had two systems of metronomy—viz., by the " heavy mina " and the " light mina," the one being twice the weight or the other ; but there is nothing to show that the *abnu rabitu*, or " grand weight," of the Code had anything to do with this. The *abnu çikhritu*, or " little weight," was a third of a shekel. Mr. C. H. W. Johns has suggested that, as the "little weight" was sixty grains, the "grand weight" may have been 120 grains.

§ 109. The XII. Tabb. (viii. 26) forbade seditious nocturnal assemblies.

§ 110. See the section "Of Priestesses."

§ 115. The XII. Tables (iii.) direct that, if a debtor cannot meet his liabilities, the creditor may arrest him and bind him with thongs, or put upon him fetters not exceeding 15lbs. weight. The debtor may live on his own means, or, if he is unable to do so, the creditor may allow him at least one pound of bread per diem. If the claim were not settled within sixty days, the debtor might be put to death or sold beyond the Tiber, after being paraded in the *comitium* on three market days and the amount of debt proclaimed. " After the third market day the creditors may cut their several portions of his body, and anyone that cuts more or less than his just share shall be held guiltless."

OF MARRIAGE.

Babylonian marriage was by contract (§ 128). Many of the contract tablets deal with this subject, and the virginity of the bride is frequently guaranteed. Consequently, the stories of Herodotus about the Babylonian women may be dismissed as idle and absurd inventions, like his other fables about Babylon ;[1] and the Code shows the importance attached to female reputation in Babylonia. The Babylonian woman was given in marriage by her father or brothers (§ 184). The suitor or his family paid a certain sum as "bride-price," the amount being often handed over in instalments (Sections 159–61). The bride's father gave her a " dowry " (*Sheriqtu*), which usually, but not necessarily, included the " bride-price " (*Tirkhatu*). The bridegroom might also make his bride a " settlement " (*Nudunnu*).

The status of the " concubine " is not clear. She does not seem to be necessarily of lower rank, like the Roman, but was a secondary spouse (§ 145). Like the chief wife, she also carried bride-price and dowry, and we may assume that she possessed the same rights as the chief wife in regard to maintenance and participation in the husband's estate.

§ 144. The cuneiform sign here translated " wife " is the one used throughout the Code

[1] *The Laws of Moses*, by Stanley A. Cook, M.A. (London, 1903), p. 101.

to denote a married woman. The precept, therefore, applies to any married woman.

§ 150. The words in brackets appear to have been accidentally omitted from the inscription.

§ 158. This refers to incest with a father's wife who is not the mother of the offender.

§ 165. A father's property was divided equally among his sons. He had no testamentary power, though he could disinherit an undutiful son (Sections 168, 169), but only under judicial direction. Daughters were provided for by their dowries. Deeds of gift made during a man's lifetime were valid against any claim made by an heir. The Code makes no provision in cases where there are no sons; but it may be taken that in such a situation the wife would inherit (Sections 172, 176).

Sections 171, 172. These paragraphs appear to have been incompletely divided by Father Scheil; but it would lead to confusion to alter the numeration.

Sections 176. By a printer's error in Father Scheil's work, two succeeding paragraphs have the same number prefixed to them.

§ 177. The word in brackets appears to have been accidentally omitted from the inscription.

OF PRIESTESSES.

Sections 178–82 relate to women under religious vows. Four of the words used are preceded by the determinative for a married woman. They are :—

NIN-AN	=	Priestess
Kallati	=	An undowered priestess
Qadishtu	=	An inferior priestess
Wife of Merodach	=	ditto

Two of the titles have merely the prefix for "woman," and they were therefore unmarried. They were the *Zikru* and the "virgin."

The priestesses of Carthage were always married; and on the Carthaginian tombstones the husband of the priestess is invariably mentioned by name. It is therefore to be expected that the Babylonian priestesses were also married. § 181 mentions virgins, but they were evidently of low rank in the hierarchy. The principal priestess is denoted by the signs NIN-AN, "Divine Lady." She was expected to lead a blameless life. She might not open a tavern, or even enter one (§ 110); and slander against a NIN-AN was severely punished (§ 127).

The priestess (NIN-AN) had received a dowry from her father (Sections 178, 179). Where no dowry was given (§ 180) the NIN-AN is replaced by the *Kallati;* so that the *Kallati* is a dowerless priestess. A *Qadishtu* is in the same predicament; but, being of lower rank, she only takes the usufruct of a third of a son's share, whereas a *Kallati* has the usufruct of a complete son's share. The "Wife of Merodach" ranked with a *Qadishtu*, except that she had the power to bequeath her share of her father's estate.

The virgin ranks with a *Qadishtu.*

The unmarried *Zikru* "devotee" may receive a dowry upon entering a religious life (Sections 178, 179), or she may not (§180). Her children were not acknowledged (Sections 187, 192, 193). *Zakaru* is a root found in Syriac, Hebrew, and Arabic, as well as in Assyrian, with the meaning of "male," "name," or "memorial." Father Scheil takes it with its determinative prefix, reads *zinnishat zikru,* and renders "female of the male," though in such case it should be *zinnishat zikri.* Dr. Winckler makes it "courtesan." The Rev. Mr. Johns, of Cambridge, reads *zinnishtu zikru* (which is more in accordance

with the text), and renders it " vowed woman."
This is practically the same as our rendering
"devotee."

§ 187. *Ner-se-ga* is an unknown class.
From § 193 it appears to have been a man;
from §187 he was attached to the governor's
palace. His children were not acknowledged,
nor allowed to recognise their parentage
(Sections 192, 193).

§ 188. A "son of the people," *mar ummia,*
was an artisan (see § 274).

Sections 196, 197, 200. This is the *Lex
talionis*. The XII. Tabb. (viii. 2) "If a man
breaks another's limb, and does not com-
promise the injury, he shall be liable to
retaliation." (viii. 3) " For breaking a bone
of a free man the penalty shall be 300 *ases* of
bronze; of a slave, 150 *ases*."

§ 202. The word translated " body " may
mean a part of the viscera, or, as Father
Scheil renders it, "brain." The Section may
be compared with XII. Tabb. (viii. 4), which
prescribe a penalty of twenty-five *ases* of
bronze for a personal injury or affront.

§ 215. The word *nagabti,* translated
" tumour," is of uncertain significance,
though, as the root has the meaning of

"hollow," it is most likely to be connected with an abscess, ulcer, or tumour. Father Scheil suggests that, as the word is several times used in connection with the eye, it may refer to the operation for cataract; but a successful operation for cataract does not always completely restore the sight of the eye, owing to the necessary removal of part of the cornea, and the Babylonians had no lenses to correct such a defect. The patient might consider his eye destroyed because he was unable to see as well as before, and the surgeon would thus be blamed for a perfectly successful operation. It would, therefore, seem better to understand *nagabti* as a tumour. Where the tumour involved the eye the surgeon could claim his fee on the higher scale for a successful operation.

§ 226. The *gallabu* combined the professions of barber and brander. His services were sometimes required in courts of law (§ 127).

§ 234. The tonnage of Babylonian boats was expressed in *gur*, the *gur* being about a ton and a fifth. Boats were built from five *gur* upwards, and in one of his letters Hammurabi speaks of a ship of seventy-five *gur*, which must have been nearly equal in size to a modern vessel of 100 tons burthen. The boat in the text is of sixty *gur*, and we have translated " sixty-ton boat " for brevity.

§ 236. The word *ultebi* evidently means " sunk," not merely " run aground " (see § 238).

§ 240. It being quite uncertain what these terms signify, they are left untranslated. By § 276 a *makhirtu* was a small vessel, for it could be hired for 2½ grains of silver; whereas a sixty-ton boat earned thirty grains of silver a day.

§ 241. Oxen were exempted from distraint as being absolutely necessary for agriculture ; therefore, the same penalty is inflicted as in the case of illegal distraint (§ 114).

§ 249. Mundane events being under the control of the gods, anything inexplicable was put down to the stroke of a god (compare Sections 45, 48).

§ 254. If the *metayer* has ill-used the oxen so that they cannot do the work, he must execute the field labour with the *marru*, a kind of hoe still in use in Mesopotamia under the same name. This would entail great manual exertion on his part.

§ 256 shows that a man's superior was usually expected to assist him in fines and liabilities. In fact, the penalties laid down in the Code

could be met in no other way, for they would
be quite beyond the means of labourers and
small farmers. Mr. Stanley A. Cook shows
from actual contract-tablets that when a man
hired himself out he had to find a guarantor.[1]
Dr. Winckler supposes the law to indicate a
man's " village community "; but it does not
appear that such communities existed in Babylonia—in fact, the whole tenour of the Code is
opposed to such a theory, for it only contemplates that the landholder will make bargains
with *individual* tenants and workpeople.

Sections 259, 260. The objects mentioned
in these two paragraphs refer to irrigating
machines, not mill wheels.

§ 273. The Babylonian year began in
Nisan, or April, and the fifth month was
Ab, or August. Consequently, the first five
months were the period of the hardest agri-
cultural work, and the workman (literally
" man of hire ") received increased pay.

§ 274. Just at this point there is a fissure in
the stone where the pillar was broken across,
and the columns of cuneiform characters are
badly mutilated.

§ 280. " Children of the land " would mean

---

[1] *Laws of Moses*, p. 174.

natives of Babylonia. As a Babylonian could only be held in bondage three years (§ 117), he was emancipated under the circumstances stated in the text.

§ 282. The loss of an ear was the usual punishment of a refractory slave (see § 205).

In his final peroration Hammurabi says, "I have not reposed myself upon my side "—*i.e.*, he had not given himself up to sloth, but had been active for the good of his people. Then, as is usual in monuments of antiquity, the king threatens, with the most frightful curses, anyone who alters or damages the pillar.

OF HOMICIDE.

It is worthy of note that the Code makes no provision for wilful homicide except in Sections 24 and 153. It would therefore appear that this crime was treated as extra-judicial. In § 153 it is enacted that a woman guilty of murdering her husband shall be impaled ; but this may merely mean that her body was to be impaled, and gives us no information as to the method or rule of execution. In § 24 the relatives of a man murdered by bandits receive one mina of silver (twice the price of accidental homicide, § 207). This would seem to show that the institution of blood-money was recognised in Babylonia. On the other hand, manslaughter rendered a man subject to the *lex talionis* (Sections 229, 210, 230), and this certainly indicates that among the Babylonians, as among other ancient peoples, homicide was dealt with by the *vendetta*. In the Old Testament it was one of the duties of the *goel*, the next of kin, to avenge murder; and the Pentateuch is quite uncompromising upon the subject. Exodus xxi. 12, 14, denies all sanctuary to the murderer. Deut. xix. 12 shows that the Hebrew judicial authorities had nothing to do with homicide except to hand over the criminal to the vengeance of the *goel ha-dam*. And Num. xxxv. 19, 21, 31, reiterates the command that the "avenger of blood" shall slay the murderer whenever and wherever he may meet him, and that no compensation is to be accepted. In the same way, therefore, it is pretty certain that in Babylonia wilful homicide was a family matter with which the judicature was not allowed to interfere. If it had been customary to compound for the crime, we may be sure that the legislator would have made some attempt to regulate the blood-price, as is done in the other cases. The silence of the Code, therefore, is significant. The El Amarna letters demonstrate the existence of the blood-feud in Babylonia, for Burna-Buriash writes to Amenophis IV. that, if the blood of his messengers who have been slain in Canaan is not requited, then Egyptian messengers may be slain in retaliation.[1]

[1] *Records of the Past*, New Series, vol. iii., p. 66.

CHAPTER VI.

THE LAWS OF MOSES

THE Sacred Books of the Jews are written in the language called "Hebrew." This language was not confined to the Jewish community, but was the common tongue of all the ancient inhabitants of Palestine; for the inscription of Mesha, king of Moab (about 850 B.C.), is a specimen of Hebrew, as are also the lapidary memorials of the Phenicians, who dwelt on the coast of the Mediterranean. The earliest independent references to the land of Palestine are to be found upon the monuments of the Egyptian kings Thothmes III. and Rameses II.[1] These monuments contain lists of names of Syrian localities; and, as far as Palestine is concerned, these names agree in character with the later nomenclature of the country—that is to say, they are to be explained by the Hebrew language. The Hebrew-speaking peoples, therefore, must

---

[1] *Records of the Past*, New Series, vol. v., p. 54; vol. vi., p. 19.

have been settled in Palestine for a very long period to have so completely coloured the topography in this way; in fact, we are justified in saying that Hebrew had been spoken in the country from time immemorial.

In the year 1887 a discovery was made at Tell-el-Amarna, in Egypt, of a large number of clay tablets, inscribed with cuneiform characters. These tablets proved to be communications addressed to the Egyptian kings Amenophis III. and Amenophis IV. The correspondents of these monarchs comprised Assur-uballit, king of Assyria, Burna-Buriash, king of Babylonia, and a number of Syrian notables. It need hardly be said that the language employed on the letters of the kings of Assyria and Babylonia was the one known as Semitic-Babylonian. But there were a number of the tablets addressed from places in Palestine; and these Palestinian tablets were in Semitic-Babylonian also! We have just seen that the indigenous language of Palestine was Hebrew. How comes it, therefore, that these Palestinian letters were written in a foreign tongue? The only reply can be that Hebrew was at that time an *illiterate language*. If there had been any means of writing Hebrew, we may be sure that the

princes of Palestine would never have gone to
the trouble of getting their messages translated into Babylonian, and written down in
the intricate and difficult cuneiform script.   In
other cases where previously illiterate nations
came into contact with the cuneiform method
of writing, and adopted it, they did not
employ the foreign language very long; but
very quickly adapted the cuneiform syllabary
to their own tongue.   A notable instance of
this is met with in the Proto-Armenian inscriptions of Van.[1]   In the Tell-el-Amarna
correspondence, the king of Mitanni (a district in Mesopotamia near Carchemish) occasionally employed his own language as well
as Semitic; and the Persians at a later period
not only appropriated the Babylonian style of

[1] "Since the publication of my Memoir on ' The Cuneiform Inscriptions of Van Deciphered and Translated' in
the *Journal of the Royal Asiatic Society*, xiv. 4, 1882, we
have begun to learn something about a race of kings who
ruled on the shores of Lake Van in Armenia, from the
ninth to the seventh centuries before our era.   The founder
of the dynasty, Sarduris I., the son of Lutipris, who reigned
B.C. 833, introduced the cuneiform system of writing as
well as other elements of Assyrian culture into the country
over which he was king.   The inscriptions he has left us
are in the Assyrian language; but his successors discon-
tinued the use of a foreign tongue, and the language of
their texts is invariably their native one."—Prof. A. H.
Sayce, in *Records of the Past*, New Series, vol. i., p. 163.

writing, but developed a new system of cuneiform of their own. The inference is, therefore, that the Hebrew princes had not been familiar with cuneiform very long, or they would have applied it to their own language in similar fashion to other nations. The oldest known specimens of written Hebrew are the Baal Lebanon Bronzes.[1] *These are in alphabetic writing.* It is obvious that no people that once employed the alphabetic character would ever abandon it for the cumbrous cuneiform; and therefore the alphabet cannot have been known in the Tell-el-Amarna period. And when once it was introduced we may be sure that there was no further possibility of cuneiform being applied for the writing of Hebrew. Even Semitic Babylonian records appear to have been rare in Palestine, for only three examples have yet been unearthed there—namely, the tablet discovered by Dr. Bliss at Tell-el-Hesy in 1892 ; and the two found by Dr. Sellin at Taanach in 1903.[2] Seeing that baked tablets of clay are practically indestructible, it is evident that many more would have come to light ere this

---

[1] *The History of the Alphabet*, by Isaac Taylor, vol. i., p. 213.

[2] *Orientalischer Litteraturzeitung*, Aug., 1903, col. 321.

if the custom of employing them had ever been largely followed in the country.

There is one thing, however, which the tablets of Tell-el-Amarna make quite clear, and that is that at the time they were written there were no such people as the Israelites in Palestine; for the data they furnish cannot be squared with the statements of the books of Joshua and Judges. It has been pointed out in Chapter III., p. 15, that, according to the testimony of Nabonidus, Burna-Buriash reigned over Babylon 700 years after Hammurabi; and as Burna-Buriash was the author of some of the Tell-el-Amarna letters it follows, therefore, that Hammurabi must have lived at least 700 years before the appearance of the Jews in Canaan.

It is hardly necessary nowadays to insist upon the fact that the well-known narratives of Genesis, such as the two accounts of the Creation and the stories of the Flood, are merely excerpts from Babylonian cosmogony and Babylonian mythology. The discovery of the great Code raises the very natural question as to whether the *legislation* of the Pentateuch is not also of Babylonian origin. It is true that the Jews attributed their legislation to Moses; but Moses (if he ever had any

real existence) must have lived seven centuries
later than the Babylonian lawgiver.   Even in
the life-legend of the Hebrew legislator we are
confronted with Babylonian elements, for the
story told of the infancy of Moses is also
related of the famous Babylonian monarch
Shargani-shar-ali, or Sargon of Agade, who
flourished about 3800 B.C., and who is said to
have been exposed in an ark of bulrushes
upon the river Euphrates, whence he was
rescued, and grew up to be ruler of all
Babylonia.

Modern scholarship has dissected the
Hebrew Pentateuch into several superposed
layers ranging in date from about the eighth
century B.C. to the time of Alexander the
Great.   The details of this dissection have
been stated with great caution and moderation
by Dr. S. R. Driver,[1] and need not be repeated
here; but they establish the existence in the
so-called Books of Moses of at least four
systems of legislation, in the following order:—

The Book of the Covenant = Exod. xx.-
xxiii. 33 (to which is related Exod. xxxiv.
11–26).

The Book of Deuteronomy.

[1] *An Introduction to the Literature of the Old Testament,*
fifth edition (Edinburgh, 1894).

The Law of Holiness = Levit. xvii.–xxvi.

The Priests' Code = The balance of the "Mosaic" Legislation.

The *Priests' Code* is the latest and most important constituent of the Pentateuch. It cannot be earlier than the time of Ezra, while it received additions at even later dates.

The *Law of Holiness* is a distinct Code in itself, resembling the other two previous codes by opening with sacrificial instructions, and closing with a parenetic exhortation.[1] The closest affinities of this stratum of the Pentateuch are with the prophet Ezekiel, to whose time it probably belongs.

Deuteronomy is evidently the "Book of the Law" which Hilkiah, the High-priest of Jerusalem, professed to have found in the Temple in the eighteenth year of Josiah (*i.e.*, 621 B.C.).

This leaves us with the *Book of the Covenant* as the earliest extant example of Hebrew legislation. Professor W. Robertson Smith[2] styled Exod. xx.–xxiii. "the First Legislation"; later critics have preferred the term *Bundesbuch*, or "Book of the Covenant."

---

[1] Driver, p. 44.

[2] *The Old Testament in the Jewish Church* (Edinburgh, 1881), p. 316.

This "book" appeared so important to the author of Exodus that he represented it as having been dictated to Moses by Yahveh himself from the mount of Sinai, to the accompaniment of smoke, fire, trumpets, thunders and lightnings, and every circumstance that could contribute to the awful and solemn character of the revelation. This reverence for the "book," however, was not shared by other Israelites, for the author of Deuteronomy had no scruple whatever in endeavouring to supersede it by a rival code, and Professor W. R. Smith gave a table to show "how completely Deuteronomy covers the same ground as the First Legislation."[1] Even in Exodus itself we see that the scribes had no hesitation in tampering with the text, for it is obvious that xx. 18 follows immediately after xix. 25, the intermediate "Ten Words" being an interpolation. Furthermore, if the Ten Words had formed part of the original text of Exodus, there would have been no necessity for xx. 23, which simply repeats xx. 4. In the same way xxiii. 12 would be redundant in face of xx. 9, 10.

---

[1] *O. T. J. C.*, p. 432. See also Hastings' *Dictionary of the Bible*, article " Deuteronomy."

There have been interminable discussions
upon the date and origin of the Ten Commandments, which are now inserted in the
twentieth chapter of Exodus. As, however,
the phrase " the stranger within thy gates "
(xx. 10) is distinctly Deuteronomic, we must
take it that these commandments are later
than Deuteronomy. As, furthermore, xx. 11
refers to the *six days of creation*, the passage
must be later than the first chapter of Genesis,[1]
which is part of the Priests' Code, and therefore comparatively modern. The Ten Commandments must therefore be eliminated, and
the speech of Yahveh commences at Exod.

[1] " The six days of creation " is not a Babylonian idea,
nor is it found upon the " Creation Tablets " which describe
the overthrow of Tiamat by Merodach and the subsequent
formation of the universe. As Delitzsch and Martineau
have pointed out, an attentive perusal of the first chapter
of Genesis reveals the fact that the days of creation were
no part of the original Hebrew narrative. The Elohist
account originally made the creation to take place by
eight stages—viz., Gen. i. 3, 6, 9, 11, 14, 20, 24, 26. Each
of these sections originally began with the words " and
God said," and ended with " and God saw that it was
good "; but the latter phrase has dropped out of the second
section, probably by a clerical error, though the Talmud
assures us that the words were intentionally omitted
because hell was created on that day. Consequently, the
division of the creation among the six days of the week
must have been the work of some late Sabbatarian, who
thought by that means to give a greater authority to the
old Babylonian institution of the *Sabattu*, or sabbath.

xx. 22, and extends to xxiii. 33. It consists essentially of a code of laws, mingled with exhortations.

The question now arises as to the *originality* of this Sinaitic legislation. In view of the Hammurabi Code, it was clearly unnecessary for Moses to seek for any supernatural guidance in framing a body of laws, seeing that such an excellent system had been worked out 700 years before, and the Israelites were on the eve of entering a land where the Babylonian legislation was in all probability well known. Assuming, however, that modern criticism is right, and that the laws in Exodus are no earlier than the prophets Hosea, Amos, and Micah (*i.e.*, the eighth century B.C.), we are so much the further removed from the time of Hammurabi, and so much the closer to the fresh wave of Babylonian influence which was rapidly spreading westward owing to the Assyrian conquests. It may be remarked that the arrangement of the Book of the Covenant bears a superficial resemblance to that of the Code of Hammurabi. The " Book " begins with directions as to how Yahveh is to be worshipped; then follow the laws; and finally there is an exhortation to observe these laws. The Code opens with a declaration of the

greatness of Hammurabi; then come the laws;
and lastly there is an appeal to posterity to
respect his monument and legislation. In
any case, however, if there be any relationship
between the Hebrew and the Babylonian
legislations, there is only one possible con-
clusion, and that is that the Hebrew was
borrowed from the earlier Babylonian.

THE THREE ESTATES OF ISRAEL.

We have already seen that the Babylonian
Code deals with three classes of persons—
the free man, the slave, and the *Mash-en-kak*.
In like manner the Hebrew legislation is
concerned with three classes—viz., the free
man, the slave, and the *Ger* (translated
" stranger " in the English version). The
Ger=" client " or " sojourner " was a person
intermediate between a slave and a full
citizen. The pious Israelite sometimes described himself as a *Ger* of Yahveh (Ps. xxxix.
12), and on the Phenician monuments we
have such names as Ger-Melek, Ger-Astarte,
Ger-Melqarth, etc. But while the *Mash-en-
kak* has clearly defined rights in Babylonian
Law, the Book of the Covenant merely recommends that the *Ger* shall not be wronged or

oppressed (Exod. xxii. 21, xxiii. 9). There is
a vast difference between giving a man a legal
standing and simply recommending him to
mercy. In Deuteronomy the *Ger* is still the
object of a semi-contemptuous pity; and
while the Book of the Covenant (Exod. xxii.
31) directs that flesh torn by wild animals is
to be given to dogs to eat, the more frugal
Deuteronomist allows unclean food to be
given to the *Ger*. The Priests' Code, however, shows the *Ger* on the high road to
amalgamation or emancipation, for it directs
that there shall be one law for the *Ger* and for
the freeborn Israelite (Lev. xxiv. 22; Num.
xv. 15).

THE JEWISH TRIBUNAL.

The Code of Hammurabi may be considered
to have definitely settled the true meaning of
Exod. xxi. 6, xxii. 8, 9. The Code regularly
directs that a case shall be taken *makhar ili*—
i.e., "before God" (or "before a god," for
the Babylonians were not so poverty-stricken
that they only had one God). The Book of
the Covenant in one place directs that a slave
shall be brought "unto God," and in the
other passages that litigants shall "come near
unto God." Commentators and translators

with a dread of anthropomorphism have been puzzled over these passages, and have suggested that the word *Elohim* here means "judges," as we may see by the margin of the Revised Version. But, in view of the Babylonian Code, there can be no doubt whatever that what is meant is the local altar of the deity; and in 1 Sam. ii. 25 we read of *Elohim* judging between man and man, so that the author of this part of Samuel at any rate was familiar with the idea of bringing cases "before God."

The best way to determine the relationship of the Book of the Covenant is to compare it verse by verse with the Code of Hammurabi; and, as Exod. xx. 22-26 is merely of a ritual character, we must commence our comparison with the twenty-first chapter.

§ 117. The principle of the Babylonian and Hebrew enactments is the same. In both cases the free native cannot be held in perpetual slavery. But while the Babylonian law limited the period of bondage to three years, the Hebrew extended it to six; and even this was eventually found to be too short a time to enable the average debtor to repay

Exod. xxi. 2-11

his debt. Therefore, in the Priests' Code (Lev. xxv. 39–41), the period of servitude is extended to forty-nine years, or the year of Jubilee. The lengthened period of servitude sanctioned by Hebrew law gave rise to complications not met with in the Code of Hammurabi. The latter does not anticipate that the bondmaster will find a wife for a bondsman, or that the bondmaster will seek to marry the debtor's daughter to himself or his relations. The Hebrew slave could not be sold into a foreign land, and § 280 emancipates slaves that have been conveyed into another country. The Babylonian Code is, however, more completely on the side of freedom than the Hebrew. By § 175 children of a free mother are free; by § 171 children of a free father are free; it was only when *both* parents were slaves that the children remained in the same status.

v. 12   The Babylonian Code made no provision for wilful homicide.

v. 13   The Code § 207 inflicts a fine of thirty shekels for accidental homicide.

v. 14   See v. 12.

v. 15   § 195 prescribes that a son who strikes his father loses his hand. The Hebrew law is more severe.

§ 14. Hebrew and Babylonian are in agree- v. 16
ment.

§ 192. The foster-child who denied his v. 17
foster-parents lost his tongue.

§ 206. Both codes are identical. v. 18, 19

The Babylonian Code only contemplates v. 20, 21
injuries to slaves by third parties. In § 217,
however, the owner is liable for fees for
medical attendance on a slave.

Sections 209–214 are more detailed than the v. 22-25
Hebrew, and, as the Code only recognises the
lex talionis in the case of equals (§ 200), the law
of retaliation only comes into force in case of
the death of a free woman.

The Hebrew assesses eye or tooth of slave v. 26, 27
at full value; the Babylonian at only half
(§ 199).

§ 250. Both legislations acquit the owner of v. 28
a goring ox; but the Hebrew has superposed
the Bedaween idea that the animal is
accursed. The ox is to be stoned to death,
and its flesh may not be eaten.

§ 251. The Hebrew law lays the owner of a v. 29-32
vicious ox open to the vengeance of the
relatives of the deceased, though they are
allowed to accept a ransom if they so choose.
The Babylonian fixes a penalty of thirty
shekels in case of a free man; twenty shekels

for a slave. The Hebrew assesses the slave at thirty shekels; and in all cases directs the ox to be stoned.

v. 33-36 Although the Babylonian Code does not provide for these specific instances, Sections 53–56 make a man responsible for injuries done to the property of others.

xxii. 1 § 262 would probably deal with this if it were entire. § 8 inflicts a thirty-fold penalty in the case of a free man, ten-fold in the case of a plebeian, for animals stolen from palace or temple.

v. 2-4 § 21. Both direct a thief caught in the act to be slain; but the Hebrew (like the *XII. Tabb.*) limits this to robbery by night.

v. 5 § 57. In both Codes trespass is to be paid for in kind.

v. 6 See note to xxi. 33–36.

v. 7 § 125. Both laws agree, and both leave to the depositee the duty of recovering the loss from the thief.

v. 8 § 120. In both laws the suspected depositee has to clear himself by oath " before God."

v. 9 Sections 9–13. The Babylonian is the more detailed in directing inquisition into claims for lost property. But while the Code is concerned in tracing out and identifying the original thief, the Hebrew legislator merely orders the receiver or holder of the stolen goods to refund double.

§ 266. Both laws are identical ; and in both v. 10, 11 the shepherd clears himself by oath.

§ 263. The laws again agree. v. 12

§ 244. The laws again agree. v. 13

Sections 245–8. The laws agree, but the v. 14 Babylonian is more detailed.

The Babylonian law makes no mention of v. 15 such a case as injury to an animal in charge of its owner. But it would probably take the same view. The Hebrew gloss is not very enlightening (glosses seldom are) ; but it probably means that the owner, having voluntarily put the animal to the work, he had no grievance if any ill result followed.

§ 130. The Code agrees more fully with v. 16, 17 Deut. xxii. 25, 26. The regulation in Exodus implies that the Hebrew father exacted a higher bride-price for a virgin daughter. Seduction rendered her less saleable, and therefore he was given the right to compel the seducer to marry the girl at the full price, or pay the difference in her value.

The Book of the Covenant only inhibits a v. 18 *female* sorcerer מכשפה. From Jer. xxvii. 9 it appears that male sorcerers were recognised in Israel even after the publication of Deut.

xviii. 10, which forbade them.   In Isaiah iii. 3, which is probably pre-Deuteronomic, the cunning charmer and the skilful enchanter are reckoned among the notables, and the deprivation of the services of these sorcerers is held up as a terrible punishment.

v. 19   Not in Babylonian Code.

v. 20   The Babylonian Code nowhere inculcates religious persecution.

v. 21   The Hebrew merely recommends the *Ger* to the mercy of the Israelite, while the Babylonian Code contains a series of regulations in regard to the rights of the *Mash-en-kak*.

v. 22–24   Widows and orphans are left in the Hebrew to the mercy of relations, and it appears from the complaints of the prophets, Isaiah i. 23, Ezek. xxii. 7, Mal. iii. 5, etc., that these unfortunates received scant justice in Israel.

v. 25–27   § 241. The Hebrew forbids distraint upon necessary clothing, but inflicts no penalty in case of infraction.   Deut. xxiv. 6 forbids distraint upon a quern or quern-stone, but likewise inflicts no penalty.   The Babylonian extends the provision to plough oxen, and enforces the regulation by fine.

v. 28–31   There are no religious ordinances in the Babylonian Code.

xxiii. 1–3, 6–8   Sections 3, 4, and 5. While the Hebrew is

merely rhetorical, the Babylonian makes practical provisions.

The rest of Exod. xxiii. is either religious or aphoristic, and therefore presents no analogy with an established code of legislation.

There is no need to suppose that the promulgation of the Book of the Covenant put a stop to the influence of external codes upon Hebrew law, and we actually find precepts in the later legislation of the Pentateuch which recall ordinances of the Hammurabi Code that are neglected in Exodus. Thus :—

§ 3 is in greater agreement with Deut. xix. 15–21 than Exod. xxiii. 1–8, to which we have compared it.

§ 59 may have inspired Deut. xx. 19.

§ 60 prescribes that, when an arboriculturist undertakes to plant an orchard, he is to enjoy the fruit for four years, and in the *fifth* year the owner comes in and takes his share. Lev. xix. 23–25 reads very much like a blundering reminiscence of this ordinance. For three years the yield of the orchard is *tabu*, the fourth year's crop is sacred, and not until the *fifth* year (as in the Babylonian) does the owner appropriate the fruit.

§ 129 agrees with Deut. xxii. 22.

K

§ 132. Numb. v. 11–31 is essentially the same; and in both cases the woman is directed to undergo an ordeal by water. The Babylonian Holy River, however, was out of the question, for rivers are rare in Palestine. It is therefore replaced by the "water of jealousy."

Sections 154–58. The Hebrew laws of incest, omitted in the Book of the Covenant, are to be found in Deut. xxvii. 20, 22, 23, and Lev. xviii. 6–18.

Several of the usages referred to in the legends of the Hebrew patriarchs are now seen to be in accordance with the Hammurabi Code. Thus in Gen. xvi. 3 the barren Sarai gives her maid Hagar to Abram for the purpose of raising children. In Gen. xxx. 3 Jacob's wife Rachel acts in the same manner; while xxx. 9 relates the same thing of Leah. All this is in strict conformity with Sections 144–46 of the Code. In Gen. xvi. 4–16 Hagar plumed herself upon her superiority to her mistress, as in § 146, and Sarai "dealt hardly with her," as she was entitled to do by the Code. Hagar ran away, and was sent back home by the "angel of the Lord," who directed her to submit herself to her mistress. If the angel had been a police officer of

Hammurabi, he could hardly have acted otherwise.

When Jacob kept the flocks of Laban (Gen. xxxi. 38–40) he prided himself upon having observed the Babylonian laws laid down in Sections 262–67, and upon the fact that he had not availed himself of § 266 for the purpose of clearing himself by oath in the case of damage by wild animals. Laban, however, did not regulate his wages by § 261.

The marriage customs of the Hebrews, though not expressly regulated by law, are in general agreement with Babylonian ideas. Exod. xxii. 15 speaks of the bride-price, or *Mohar* (mistranslated "dowry" in the English version). The enamoured Shechem understood perfectly well that a bride-price would be expected for Dinah (Gen. xxxiv. 12), and offered any desired amount. And in 1 Sam. xviii. 25–27, Saul having desired a peculiar bride-price for his daughter Michal, David duly procured it, and wedded the lady.

In Jud. i. 15, and the parallel narrative in Josh. xv. 19, we have the only mention in the Old Testament of a dowry given with a daughter, it being called a *berakah* or " blessing," and not being very clearly distinguished from a mere gift from a father to his daughter.

Lastly, in Gen. xxxiv. 12 Shechem promises a *matthan*, or "gift," corresponding with the Babylonian *nudunnu*—*i.e.*, a marriage settlement. It seems, therefore, that all the ordinances of Babylonian marriage were recognised in Israel, although the bride-price was the only one that received any great amount of attention.

These resemblances should be decisive. In our notes on the Hammurabi Code we took occasion to compare it with an independent system of legislation, the Laws of the Twelve Tables; and the similarities discovered were neither numerous nor striking. On the other hand, in the comparison of the Hebrew Book of the Covenant with the Babylonian Code, the resemblances are simply overwhelming. Out of thirty-two ordinances, twenty-one are in accord with the Babylonian, most being practically identical, and the others being quite in the Babylonian spirit. The inference is, therefore, that *the Hammurabi Code must have been the immediate or remote progenitor of the Hebrew legal system.*

For the sake of simplicity we have so far regarded the "Book of the Covenant" as though it were a homogeneous composition; but it must be evident to every attentive student that it is nothing of the kind. The differences of style observable in it have been investigated by several eminent critics, whose conclusions have been summarised by Professor G. F. Moore.[1] For our purpose, however, it will be sufficient to indicate merely a few of the peculiarities of the "Book." The way in which chapter xxi. commences would lead one to expect a carefully-digested corpus of law. First we have stated the hypothetical case of the purchase of a Hebrew slave, and then comes an orderly consideration of the various contingencies arising therefrom. But this complete and methodical treatment is not maintained. The laws are mixed confusedly together, so that xxi. 22-25 has become inserted in the middle of a section dealing with an entirely different subject (verses 20, 21, and 26, 27), and after xxii. 17 the ordinances become a mere jumble. In fact, these three chapters of Exodus look more like the wreck of a Code than an orderly statement of one.

[1] See his article "EXODUS (BOOK)" in the *Encyclopædia Biblica*, edited by the Rev. T. K. Cheyne, vol. ii. (London, 1901).

There is also some difference in the way in which the several laws are stated. The greater part are put hypothetically as in the Code of Hammurabi (for the Babylonian *shumma amelu*, "if a man," answers pretty closely to the Hebrew וכי איש, "and if a man"), but in other instances they are categorical. Thus xxii. 18 commences "thou shalt not," and xxii. 19 "whosoever lieth," in an entirely different style to the hypothetically stated enactments. Even these latter are stated variably, some being addressed to the pronoun of the second person, and others (in the style of the Babylonian Code) being referred to the third person. Thus xxii. 25, "If thou lend money," should be contrasted with xxii. 1, "If a man shall steal an ox." A further peculiarity in these two hypotetics is that in the one God is represented as speaking directly, while in the other he is referred to as a third party. Thus xx. 25, "If thou make *me* an altar of stone"; but in xxi. 6, "his master shall bring him unto *God*." If, now, we separate the sections which speak of the third person, in the Babylonian style, we shall find they consist of the following : xxi. 1–11, 14, 18–36 ; xxii. 1–17 ; and these are the passages that agree best with the Code of Hammurabi ! It is evident,

therefore, that the verses in question are
fragments of an early Hebrew book of laws
which was derived from the Babylonian Code.
The fragments are preceded and introduced
by the words, "And these the *mishpatim*
which thou shall set before them." The word
משפטים *mishpatim*, "judgments," answers to
the Babylonian *dinani*, for the Semitic root
דין = to judge, only exists in Hebrew in
poetical passages, being replaced for ordinary
purposes by שפט, which is peculiar to the
Phenician branch. Hammurabi calls his
Code *Dinani mesharim*, "judgments of
justice"; the Hebrew legislator calls the old
Hebrew Code *mishpatim* "judgments"; and
the Psalmist speaks of the משפטי צדק, "judgments of justice," just like the Babylonian
(Ps. cxix. 7, 62, 164); so that the technical
phrases are practically identical.

The discovery of the Code of Hammurabi,
therefore, enables us to place the criticism of
the Book of the Covenant upon a fresh and
sound basis. It is now perfectly clear that
the compiler of the "book" adopted such of
the older laws as suited his purpose, and
added to them sundry regulations of a ritual
character, together with precepts of the kind
that have been popular with moralists of all

ages, from the counsels of Ptah-hotep[1] (3,500 B.C.) to the copy-books of the twentieth century. The science of jurisprudence must have been at a very low ebb in Palestine when such a compilation as the Book of the Covenant was possible. The laws themselves are treated as quite subordinate, and the interest of the compiler centres in theological matters, such as the proper methods of sacrifice and the regulation of the periodic festivals. In the later systems of Pentateuchal legislation this tendency is progressively increased. The Book of Deuteronomy cannot conceal its entire dependence upon the Book of the Covenant for its legal matter ; and the additions made are merely religious and sermonistic. Even Canon Driver sums up the characteristics of the later codes as follows :[2]

"From a literary point of view *Deuteronomy* (disregarding the few short passages belonging to P, and the two poems in chs. 32, 33) consists of a code of laws accompanied by hortatory introductions and comments."

---

[1] *The Precepts of Ptah-hotep: the Oldest Book in the World*, by M. Phillipe Virey. *Records of the Past*, new series, vol. iii., p. 16.

[2] Article "LAW" in the *Dictionary of the Bible*, edited by James Hastings, vol. iii. (Edinburgh, 1900).

" We come next to the *Law of Holiness* (H) (Lv. 17–26). This consists substantially of an older body of laws, which have been arranged by a later editor in a parenetic setting, the whole thus formed being afterwards incorporated in P, with additions and modifications, designed for the purpose of harmonising it more completely with the system and spirit of P.......The original nucleus of H, when compared with the Book of the Covenant, will be seen to deal very much less fully with civil and criminal law. The only regulations relating to criminal law are those in 24₁₇₋₂₁. Those in ch. 25 might be classed as belonging formally to civil law, but they are regarded more properly as expressions of religious or humanitarian principle."

" The legislation of the *Priests' Code* properly so called (P) is confined almost entirely to ceremonial observances, especially those relating to sacrifice and purification."

In other words, the successive codes of the Pentateuch display greater and greater sacerdotalism as time goes on. It was entirely owing to the influence of the Babylonian Code of Hammurabi that the religious system of the Old Testament was cast into a legal form at all. The Hebrew language itself

bears witness to the knowledge of codes of
law engraved upon stone, like the pillar found
by M. de Morgan at Susa.   Dr. Driver,[1] who
of course knew nothing at that time of the
Hammurabi Code, points out that the Hebrew
חק, *khoq*, and חקה, *khuqqah*, "statute" or
"ordinance," are derived "from חקק, *to cut
in, inscribe, engrave*, and therefore denote properly something *engraven* on stone or other
durable surface, though applied in usage to any
kind of fixed ordinance.   It was a common
practice in antiquity to engrave laws upon slabs
of stone or metal and to set them up in some
public place—*and the same custom is presupposed in the use of these two words in
Hebrew*."   Hence, therefore, when the Elohist
writer of Exodus wished to describe the legislation which he alleged had been super-
naturally delivered to Moses, the legislation
presented itself to his mind as something
engraven upon stone, upon "the two tables
of the testimony," as the English Version
calls them—though עדות is more correctly
"precept" or "law."   "Tables that were
written on both their sides; on the one side
and on the other were they written.   And the

---

[1] Article "LAW" in the *Dictionary of the Bible.*

tables were the work of God, and the writing was the writing of God" (Exod. xxxii. 15, 16).

The Israelites did not preserve *all* the Babylonian laws; some were inapplicable, others implied a more advanced state of civilisation and morality than was to be found in the kingdoms of Israel and Judah.

The military regulations (Sections 26–41) did not obtain in Israel, because, as far as we know, the kings had no bodies of feudal vassals settled upon crown lands; although they did have bands of foreign mercenaries in their pay (2 Sam. xx. 7). Every able-bodied Israelite was expected to serve as a soldier, and to appear fully armed whenever called out by general levy (1 Sam. xi. 7).

The land regulations (Sections 42–56) are not represented in the Pentateuchal legislation, although there were large landholders (Is. v. 8) who must have farmed out their estates; and there was some amount of irrigation, though, of course, not on the scale practised in the valley of the Euphrates. Sections 60–65 have also disappeared from Hebrew jurisprudence, with the exception of the apparent reminiscence in Lev. xix. 23–25, of which we have already spoken.

The Jews of the Old Testament were not a

mercantile race, hence Sections 100–107 were
unnecessary. Agriculture was the staple
industry, and all commerce was in the hands
of the Phenicians; Isaiah xxiii. 8 even using
the word "Canaanite" as a synonym for
merchant.

The most noteworthy omission, perhaps, is
in regard to the laws of inheritance. The
provisions of the Hammurabi Code seem very
complete and very equitable ; but the Hebrew
laws are just the reverse. We can only learn
that Israelitish sons divided the paternal
possessions equally among themselves, except
that the eldest-born took a double share (Deut.
xxi. 15–17). Daughters only inherited upon
failure of sons ; and if there were neither sons
nor daughters, then the brother of the deceased
succeeded (Num. xxvii. 4–11). In any case,
the widow had no claim on the estate. In
early times, at any rate, she was herself considered part of the property of the deceased,
and dealt with accordingly; as was the custom
among the heathen Arabs down to the advent
of Muhammad (2 Sam. xvi. 20, iii. 7), and
the tenth commandment enumerates the wife
together with the house, the ox, the ass, and
the other property of one's neighbour. Even
the Book of the Covenant has no provision

for the widow and the orphan—they are merely recommended to mercy (Exod. xxii. 22) like the *Ger* or stranger; and we may see by the frequent prophetical denunciations that the condition of the widow and the fatherless was a standing grievance in Israel. A comparison of Babylonian law with Hebrew custom will show how far the Jews had fallen below the moral standard of the subjects of Hammurabi.

Adoption, which occupies such a large place in the Code (Sections 185-193), is not referred to in the Jewish Law; but is replaced by the curious provision of the Levirate, which treats the wife as a mere child-bearing machine (Deut. xxv. 5-10).

The Navigation Laws (Sections 234-240) were, of course, useless to the Israelites, who were not a maritime people. And the scales of fees and wages would be unenforceable out of Babylonia itself.

As already indicated, the *additions* of the Hebrew legislators were almost entirely of a theological character. The basic ideas of the Hammurabi Code are civil right and solid justice; and, considering the times and the circumstances, these are very well realised by the Code. The king makes much of his

devotion to the gods and the blessings they
have bestowed upon him ; but theology is
rigidly excluded from the Code itself. The
deities are only called in to decide by the
Ordeal in cases where human insight fails
(Sections 2 and 132), or to guarantee an oath
where human evidence is wanting. In the
Pentateuch, on the other hand, the theological
interest is paramount. The principle of
religious persecution is introduced from the
very first, being inculcated even in the Book
of the Covenant; whereas religious persecution was entirely unknown in Babylonia, not
only in the Code of Hammurabi, but throughout the whole range of cuneiform literature, as
far as we are acquainted with it at present.
Num. xxxi. 17–24 is a typical instance of
the ideal Pentateuchal combination of blood-
thirstiness and ceremonial zeal ; and one of
the objects of the completed Torah is the
establishment of a theological reign of terror.
The same penalty is prescribed for petty
infractions of ritual as for the gravest crimes ;
and the *Priests' Code* is a wearisome litany of
" that soul shall be cut off from his people."
Unauthorised compounding of oil or incense
is punishable with death (Exod. xxx. 33, 38),
so is neglect of the Passover (Num. ix. 13),

Sabbath-breaking (Exod. xxxv. 2), or even doing "aught with an high hand" (Num. xv. 30). The fierce and senseless intolerance of the Laws of Moses forms a significant contrast to the judicial dignity of the Laws of Hammurabi.

Appendix A.

THE FIRST DYNASTY OF BABYLON

ALTHOUGH we call the Southern Euphrates Valley by the name of Babylonia, Babylon was not always the capital of the country. In the earliest period the great cities were more or less independent, and every now and then one or other rose to pre-eminence, and acted as suzerain over the others for a greater or lesser period of time. These struggles eventually resulted in the supremacy of the king of Babylon ; and we have described in Chapter III. how this supremacy was finally established by the overthrow of Rim-Sin by Hammurabi. Babylon thereafter remained the capital of the country until 538 B.C., when Nabonidus, the last native monarch, was deposed by Cyrus the Great.

In 1881 Dr. Pinches published a cuneiform tablet which, in its complete state, gave lists of the kings of the various Babylonian dynasties. It was then found that Hammurabi was not the founder of a dynasty, but was the sixth member of a line of kings reigning in the city of Babylon. The family of Hammurabi is therefore styled the First Dynasty of Babylon.[1] This dynastic tablet has, however, been supplemented by other records detailed by Dr. King in vol. iii. of his *Letters of Hammurabi*.

Although the succession of the First Dynasty of Babylon and the lengths of the individual reigns are thus determined, there is as yet no certainty as to the dates when these kings flourished. The nearest approximation is to be derived from an inscription of the Assyrian king Assurbanipal (668–626 B.C.).[2] and two inscriptions of Nabonidus, the last king of Babylon (555–538 B.C.).[3]

Assurbanipal informs us that, in the early part of the year corresponding with 652 B.C., he sent an embassy to the king of Elam, demanding the restitution of a venerated image of Nana, the goddess of Erech, which had been carried away to Susa 1,635 years before by " Kudur-Nankhundi, the Elamite,

---

[1] *Records of the Past*, New Series, vol. i., p. 13.

[2] *History of Assurbanipal*, by George Smith (London, 1871), p. 250 and p. 381.

[3] *Historische Texte des neubabylonischen Reichs.* Schrader's *Keilinschriftliche Bibliothek* (Berlin, 1890), Band iii., 2 Hälfte, pp. 91 and 96.

who the worship of the great gods did not fear." The deportation of Nana thus took place in 2287 B.C., and therefore a serious invasion of Southern Babylonia must have been made by the Elamites in that year. It is tempting to link this event with the fact that Rim-Sin was of *Elamite* descent. His father, Kudur-Mabug, was "*adda*" of Emutbal and Martu. Emutbal was a province of Elam; but he could only have gained the dominion over Martu (Southern Babylonia) by conquest. As Rim-Sin reigned at least thirty-seven years (see p. 18), and was overthrown in the thirty-first year of Hammurabi, he must have commenced his sovereignty seven years before the latter monarch. To this must be added the princedom of his father; but we have no knowledge as to how long Kudur-Mabug ruled over Martu. From the lack of monuments it may have been only a few years.

Nabonidus, the last king of Babylon, devoted himself very largely to renovating the ancient temples of his dominions. Among others, he rebuilt the temple of Anunit at Sippara, and we may quote from his cylinder inscription :—

" For Anunit, the mistress of battle, bearer

of the bow and quiver, who fulfils the command of Bel, her father, who sweeps away the foe, who destroys the wicked, who marches before the gods, who at sunrise and sunset has blessed my endeavours, E Ulbar, her temple which is in Sippara of Anunit, which for 800 years, since the time of Shaga-shalti-Buriash, king of Babylon, son of Kudur-Bel, no king had built, its old founda-tion-stone I sought, and I saw, I examined; and upon the foundation-stone of Shagashalti-Buriash, the son of Kudur-Bel, I laid its foundation and made firm its brickwork. This temple I built anew, I completed its design."

Thus Shagashalti-Buriash lived 800 years before Nabonidus—say, 1345 B.C. He was a member of a dynasty of Kassite kings which ruled in Babylon some five or six hundred years.

Another monarch of the same dynasty is mentioned in a further inscription of Nabonidus, discovered at Ur:—

" The foundation-cylinder of Hammurabi, the ancient king, who, 700 years before Burna-Buriash had built E Babbara, and the tower, upon the old foundation for Shamash, I looked upon it and I feared."

Burna-Buriash, therefore, lived 700 years
after Hammurabi; but the question remains,
what was the date of Burna-Buriash? We
can only say that this monarch was one of
the correspondents of Amenophis III. and
Amenophis IV. in the Tell-el-Amarna tablets,
and these Egyptian kings reigned about
1450 B.C. Consequently, the date of Hammurabi was somewhere about 2150 B.C.
Nabonidus speaks in round numbers, and we
cannot be absolutely certain for a year or two.
This date of 2150 B.C. does not synchronise
with the figures derived from the invasion of
Kudur-Nankhundi in 2287 B.C.; but at the
same time it must be admitted that the
chronology of this period is so entirely hypothetical that the latter date is by no means
excluded.

Nabonidus seems to have been in possession
of trustworthy information in regard to the
reigns of his predecessors from very early
times, and where it has been possible to check
his figures the dates mentioned in his inscriptions have proved correct. The Assyrian
king, Assurbanipal, must also have had
equally good authority for his chronological
calculations; and it may, therefore, be
expected that further discoveries will enable

us to settle the exact period of Hammurabi's reign. But for the present it will be seen that the data are much too vague.

However, if we assume that the reign of Hammurabi ended in 2150 B.C., we get the following scheme for the first dynasty of Babylon, premising only that the dates B.C. are theoretical, and are merely given for convenience in reckoning:—

B.C.

2295	Sumu-abu, founder of the dynasty, reigned 14 years			
2281	Sumu-la-ilu,	his son,	,,	36 ,,
2245	Çabium,	his son,	,,	14 ,,
2231	Apil-Sin,	his son,	,,	18 ,,
2213	Sin-muballit,	his son,	,,	20 ,,
2193	Hammurabi,	his son,	,,	43 ,,
2150	Samsu-iluna,	his son,	,,	38 ,,
2112	Abi-eshu',	his son,	,,	28 ,,
2084	Ammi-ditana,	his son,	,,	37 ,,
2047	Ammi-zaduga,	his son,	,,	22 ,,
2025	Samsu-ditana,	his son,	,,	31 ,,

11 kings of the First Dynasty of Babylon reigned 301 years

Appendix B.

GENESIS XIV.

The earlier school of Assyriologists were
led into many errors through paying too much
regard to the fables of classical writers such
as Ctesias and Herodotus. But though these
authors have long been given up as misleading,
the *ignis fatuus* of the fourteenth chapter of
Genesis still flickers over the field of Assyri-
ology. If it were not for Gen. xiv., many
commonly-made assertions would never have
been invented, and Babylonian history would
have been more sober and less imaginative.
It is difficult to understand why this chapter
should have had such a hypnotising effect, for
its fictitious nature is its most obvious charac-
teristic. The well-known Orientalist, Professor
Nöldeke, demonstrated its unhistorical nature
half a century ago, and his conclusions have
never been refuted.[1]   In fact, it is somewhat a

[1] "Die Ungeschichtlichkeit der Erzählung Gen. xiv."
Untersuchung zur Kritik des Alten Testaments, von
Theodor Nöldeke (Kiel, 1869).

slur on one's intelligence to have it presented as possessing any historical value whatever. The string of awe-inspiring names which it offers in the English version is largely due to the fact that the Hebrew is left untranslated. By rendering all the intelligible words, as is done in the following, the real character of the narrative may be better appreciated.

" And it was in the days of Amraphel, king of Shin'ar, Aryok, king of Ellasar, Kedorla'omer, king of Elam, and Tid'al, king of nations, they made war upon Son-of-Evil,[1] king of Sedom, and upon Son-of-Wickedness, king of 'Amorah, Tooth-of-the-Father, king of Earth, Shmeber, king of hyænas and king of devouring (she is small). All these confederated to the Plain of Demons (it is the Salt Sea). Twelve years they served Kedorla'omer, and thirteen years they rebelled, and in the fourteenth year came Kedorla'omer and the kings who were with him, and they smote the Shades in Astarte of the two horns and the Zuzes in them, and the Terrors in the Plain of the Cities, and the Cave-dwellers in the high rough mountain [or, high mountain of the Satyr] until the Oak of Paran which is

---

[1] The Jewish doctors themselves recognised that the ב of Bera and Birsha was the contraction for בן *ben* " son."

above the desert. And they returned, and they came to the Well of Judgment (it is holy), and they smote all the field of the Amalekites and also the Amorites, the dwellers in the Pruning of the Palm-tree."

Dr. Nöldeke points out that the Samaritan Pentateuch, instead of *Shmeber*, has שמאבד= "the name is lost," a somewhat significant reading if it be the true one. There are other variations in the Septuagint; but they probably merely indicate that the LXX. translators were puzzled over the outlandish names.

The scene in the story is laid in the Vale of *Siddim*. This should most probably be *Shedim* (the difference in the Hebrew is merely a dot on the ש)—*i.e.*, "demons," as in Deut. xxxii. 17, and Psalms cvi. 37. The foes smitten by Chedorlaomer are of a suspiciously eschatological character. The *Rephaim* are the Shades of the Dead, as in Isa. xiv. 9, Ps. lxxxviii. 10, etc. The *Emim* are the "Terrors of Death," as in Ps. lv. 4. And as the sepulchres of Palestine are almost universally rock-hewn tombs, the "cave-dwellers" would be the dead lying in such receptacles. The two-horned Astarte and the Plain of the Cities remind us that the ruler of the Babylonian Hades was the Queen *Allatu*,

who resided in a great city, or rather seven
concentric cities with separate gates through
which the dead must pass.   Shmeber, king of
hyænas and the king of devouring, gives a
ghoulish suggestion of Oriental grave-yards;
and the Zuzim and Paran and Sodom and
Gomorrah would probably be more intelligible
if we possessed a completer knowledge of
Hebrew eschatology.   The *Seir* of verse 6, in
company with the other mythological sur-
roundings, is probably the Satyr of Lev.
xvii. 7, Isa. xxxiv. 14, etc.

The forces led by Abram against these
vanquishers of phantoms were not large.
"Three hundred and eighteen" born in his
house.   And these 318 can be reduced to one,
the famous Eliezer (Gen. xv. 2).   The letters
of the Hebrew alphabet have each a numerical
value; and if we write down the name Eliezer
in Hebrew characters, and add up the
numerical values of these characters, the
result is 318 !

א	..	1
ל	.	30
י	=	10
ע	—	70
ז	=	7
ר	=	200
		———
		318

In view of all these facts, it would require a great amount of evidence to prove that there was anything of an historical nature in Gen. xiv.; and it is somewhat needless to add that no evidence has yet been offered for the historicity of this chapter. The section belongs to the Priests' Code—that is, the latest stratum of the Pentateuch; and the narrative was constructed by someone familiar with the Hebrew alphabet, for the names of the foreign kings in verse 1 are carefully arranged in the order of that alphabet; and Bera and Birsha, and Shinab and Shemeber, are coupled together because they begin with the same letter. As these people are therefore artificial in their arrangement, they are probably equally artificial in their origin ; and it is a mere waste of time to seek for them in the field of history. The kernel of the chapter is in the twentieth verse, " And he gave him a tenth of all "; and its object was thus to support the priestly impost of tithes.

Nevertheless, ever since scholars began to decipher the cuneiform inscriptions it has been a favourite, though futile, amusement to seek for names upon the monuments bearing some remote resemblance to those in Gen. xiv.; and schemes of chronology have even been framed to bring these names into accord with the age of Abraham. Seeing, however, that the age of Abraham is an exceedingly uncertain quantity, such chronologies have not been found to be of any value.

It has occasionally been announced that " Chedorlaomer, king of Elam," has been found upon the monuments; but up to the present all such discoveries have proved to be errors in reading the cuneiform.[1]

Arioch, king of Ellasar, has been at various times identified with several eastern potentates who have eventually had to be acquitted of any connection with him. The present fashion is to equate him with Rim-Sin of Larsam. It requires the eye of faith to perceive the likeness between Ellasar and Larsam. The name we transcribe " Rim-Sin " is somewhat of a cuneiform puzzle. It is found written *Rim-En-zu, Rim-Agu, Arad-En-zu,* and *Arad-Agu;* and it was at one time maintained that these were all different people, until Mr. George Smith established their identity. *En-zu,* " lord of wisdom," and *Agu,* " crowned," are both appellations of the Moon-god, Sin.

---

[1] For a recent instance see King's *Letters of Hammurabi,* vol. i., p. xviii.

In Semitic Babylonian *En-zu* is always read as *Sin*, the Moon-god; and it is to be presumed that *Agu* is to be treated in the same way. We are thus left with Rim-Sin and Arad-Sin. As the cuneiform interchanges *Rim* with the character for "servant" (in the Semitic construct case *arad*), it would appear that in this particular case *rim* is synonymous with "servant." For the purpose of comparing the name with Arioch, the first element has been read as *Eri* or *Iri*, and this procures the form Eri-Agu (or Eri-Aku), but ignores the second form of the divine name, for no one has proposed to read *Eri-En-zu*. It will be seen, therefore, that the reading *Eri-Aku* is in the highest degree precarious, and in the present state of Assyriological knowledge the only safe rendering appears to be *Rim-Sin*.

As Shinar is several times used in the Old Testament for Babylonia, or some part of it, sundry kings of Babylon have been equated with Amraphel. Hammurabi is the chief favourite at present. The first consonant of his name is the German *Ch*, very often transcribed *Kh*. Thus we get the form *Khammurabi*. Orientalists, however, prefer the phonetically superior method of employing one letter only for each sound, and write *Kh* as *ḥ*, with a diacritical mark beneath.   Hence *Hammurabi*, which need offer no difficulty if we remember that the Assyrian *h* was a guttural.   In one single case a tablet has been found to spell Hammurabi as *Ammurabi*. This, of course, is merely one of the many instances of reckless spelling on the part of the cuneiform scribes, who had no standard etymological dictionaries to guide them.   But upon this slender basis is built the theory that *Amraphe(l)* is *Ammurabi* in disguise, the *l* having been tacked on in some unaccountable manner.

It is the fourteenth chapter of Genesis which influences the bringing into the neighbourhood of the Mediterranean of the names of some of the places mentioned on Babylonian inscriptions.   Many of these names are difficult to decipher, and still more difficult to locate.   The father of Rim-Sin is called *adda Martu*, presumed to mean "*lord* of the West-land."   There was a Babylonian deity named *Martu*, so that it is improbable that the "West-land" was far from Babylonia.   But we often find in modern books that *Martu* is translated as "Phenicia" or "Syria" without a word of explanation ; and the uninstructed reader is misled into the idea that there is some certainty in making *Martu* the Far West. There is, however, nothing in the cuneiform inscriptions themselves to preclude the idea that *Martu* was simply south-western Babylonia ; and when we find, as noted on p. 21, that Siniddinam, the vassal king of Larsam, was officially styled Governor of Martu, there is hardly need to seek for the place elsewhere.

It is, therefore, quite unnecessary for us to trouble ourselves about the assertions that have been so freely made as to the alleged contemporaneity of Abram and Hammurabi ; or the presumed relations of the early Babylonian kings with Palestine. It has yet to be shown that the author of the Priests' Code (about the 5th century B.C.) possessed any knowledge of the early Babylonian history of 1,500 years before his time ; or that the kings of Elam made expeditions to smite Rephaim in this world, whatever they might do in the next.

APPENDIX C.

RELICS OF EARLIER BABYLONIAN LAWS

THE Akkadian language ceased to be spoken in Babylonia about 2000 B.C., but as its literature was the foundation of the Semitic-Babylonian culture, and as Akkadian had become a kind of sacred tongue, it was studied and taught as long as the Babylonian religion and civilisation lasted. The great text-book of the language was a series of ten or twelve tablets entitled *Ana ittishu*, "In his station," from the opening words of the first volume. The work consisted essentially of specimens of the Akkadian language, accompanied by a Semitic-Babylonian translation. Among the specimens are several paragraphs which are evidently ancient legal enactments, their antiquity being guaranteed by the fact that they are in the Akkadian language. The tablet containing these fragments of laws is numbered K 251 in the British Museum collection, and has been frequently translated and published.[1] The following version will serve to show the character of this primitive Akkadian legislation :—

1. If a son says to his father, " Thou art not my father," they shall brand him, and fetter him, and sell him as a slave for silver [compare Hamm. Code, Sections 192, 226, 146].

2. If a son says to his mother, " Thou art not my mother," his face they shall brand, from the city they shall banish him, from the house they shall drive him.

3. If a mother says to her son, " Thou art not my son," house and goods shall she forfeit.

4. If a wife hates her husband and says, "Thou art not my husband," into the river they shall throw her [compare H. Code, Sections 142, 143].

5. If a husband says to his wife, " Thou art not my wife," half a mina of silver he shall weigh out to her [compare H. Code, Sections 137–140].

6. If a man hires a slave, and he dies, or is rendered useless, or is caused to run away, or is caused to rebel, or is made ill, then for every day his hand shall measure out half a *qa* of corn [compare H. Code, Sections 245–248, 199, 252].

[1] *Trans. Socy. Bib. Archæology*, vol. viii., p. 230.

M

GENERAL INDEX

INDEX TO CODE

(The figures refer to the Sections of the Code, pp. 27-72.)

166